Autobiography

TOWARD A POETICS
OF EXPERIENCE

Janet Varner Gunn

University of Pennsylvania Press
Philadelphia   1982

Library of Congress Cataloging in Publication Data

Gunn, Janet Varner.
  Autobiography: toward a poetics of experience.

  Bibliography: p.
  Includes index.
  1. Autobiography. I. Title
CT25.G84 808'.06692 81–43521
ISBN 0–8122–7834–8   AACR2

Printed in the United States of America

For Giles

Contents

Acknowledgments

Acknowledgment plays so fundamental a part in the theory of autobiography I put forward in these pages that I pale at having to specify the enormous debt I owe to persons, places, and ideas which have contributed to my work. Short of writing my own autobiography, and even then, I am unable to name them all. I can, however, put my finger on certain places (all of them institutions of higher learning) which were home and goad to my thinking: Gettysburg College, The University of Chicago, and Duke University. Associated with these places are teachers and friends who simply cannot go unacknowledged: Ralph D. Lindeman, Katherine Taylor, and Norman Richardson; Preston Roberts, Nathan A. Scott Jr., and Joseph Sittler; Wallace Fowlie, Wesley Kort, Thomas Langford, William Poteat, and Ruel Tyson. Even more basic, because their support made these other associations possible, are Helen Mears Peterson and Marilyn Prussing Koretz.

The ideas of certain others, living and dead, have made all the difference. The Bibliography I supply at the end of this book will suggest who and what have been most formative. I trust my own use of their ideas will join, deepen, extend, and enliven the conversation they have begun. The mention of two persons, however, cannot be put off to the end. James Olney and Elizabeth W. Bruss belong right at the beginning because, without them, my own beginnings and continuings would have been so much more difficult.

James Olney has been immeasureably helpful throughout the project of this book. His *Metaphors of Self: The Meaning of Autobiography* (Princeton, 1972), more than any study I know, shows how large a subject autobiography is and, therefore, how capacious a conception the genre requires to do it justice. Not only has his own daring been inspirational; the magnanimity he demonstrated toward my work all along, even when it veered from his own, has alleviated my discouragements and fueled my resolves. I reserve a very special mention for the late Elizabeth Bruss whose generosity and keen intelligence have made, and continue to make, more difference than I can say. Certainly, her embryonic ideas about "classical autobiography" were determinative when I came to revise my manuscript. This present book, I hope, serves as a tribute to the work she was able to complete before her untimely death.

To those who read and commented on earlier versions of my manuscript, I am particularly grateful: Charles Altieri, Malcolm Call, John J. McDermott, Paul Ricoeur, Albert E. Stone, and even the unidentified reader who vexed me toward a bolder and less cluttered argument.

The day-to-day life with my husband, Giles Gunn, over the past twenty years has made the crucial difference, since his continuing encouragement has furnished the fiduciary context for my work and has demonstrated the indispensability of being "read" by another. I dedicate this book to him.

Janet Varner Gunn
Hillsborough, North Carolina

Autobiography
TOWARD A POETICS
OF EXPERIENCE

1

The Autobiographical Situation

> You need only claim the events of your life to
> make yourself yours. When you truly possess
> all you have been and done, which may take
> some time, you are fierce with reality.
> —Florida Scott-Maxwell,
> *The Measure of My Days*

While autobiography has been around for nearly
two hundred years (and, according to some, since Augustine's *Confessions*), critical interest in the genre is fairly recent. The way had to be cleared, first of all, for attending
to autobiography as literary and not just historical activity.
Both the demise of formalism (whose criteria for "literari-
ness" the unruly behavior of autobiography refused to fit)
and the expanding of literary categories to include *écriture*
as well as *belles-lettres* have opened the door to autobiography. In a recent collection of critical essays on autobiography, James Olney offers yet another reason for current interest in the genre. It arises, he suggests, from a "shift of
attention from *bios* to *autos*—from the life to the self," a shift
which, for Olney, "was largely responsible for opening
things up and turning them in a philosophical, psychologi-
cal, and literary direction."[1]

Olney's volume reflects the state of the art, as well as

1. James Olney, ed., *Autobiography: Essays Theoretical and Critical*
(Princeton: Princeton University Press, 1980), p. 19.

the major battle lines, in autobiography criticism. The largest proportion of this collection offers accounts of the discovery and exploration of what was once called the "dark continent of literature."[2] Among the essays of early colonization is Georges Gusdorf's which sets forth what he calls the "conditions" of autobiography. The emergence of the genre "becomes possible," he maintains, "only under certain metaphysical preconditions. To begin with, humanity . . . must have emerged from the mythic framework of traditional teachings and must have entered into the perilous domain of history."[3] Gusdorf dates this virtual revolution in consciousness at around the time when "[t]he idol of an objective and critical history worshipped by the positivists of the nineteenth century [had] crumbled. . . ."[4] Autobiography could emerge, then, only when men and women began to experience what Mircea Eliade has called the "terror of history."[5] To be sure, history had been "happening" long before its discovery in the nineteenth century; but it was by means of myth that human beings were able—in Eliade's word—to "tolerate" it. Autobiography, I would add, continues to make tolerable the fullest inhabiting of that perilous domain.

While the first set of essays in Olney's volume attends and contributes to the beginning of autobiography studies, the final three look toward the *finis* of the genre.[6] These last

2. Stephen A. Shapiro, "The Dark Continent of Literature: Autobiography," *Comparative Literature Studies* V (1968): 421–54.

3. Georges Gusdorf, "Conditions and Limits of Autobiography," in *Autobiography: Essays Theoretical and Critical,* p. 30.

4. Ibid., p. 40.

5. Mircea Eliade, *Cosmos and History: The Myth of the Eternal Return,* trans. Willard R. Trask (New York: Harper & Brothers, 1959).

6. Louis A. Renza, "The Veto of the Imagination: A Theory of Autobiography," Elizabeth Bruss, "Eye for I: Making and Unmaking Autobiography in Film," Michael Sprinker, "Fictions of the Self: The End of Autobiography," in *Autobiography: Essays Theoretical and Critical,* pp. 268–342.

essays cast a curious light back on the preceding ones, re-opening certain questions that may have been inadequately or prematurely closed. The contrapuntal tensions created by these two sets of essays—the one exhibiting the impulse to assemble, the other, the impulse to dismantle—furnish a seismographic report on the fault-line that divides the territory of autobiography now under such intense scrutiny. The status of the autobiographical self rests uneasily on that fault-line.

Olney provides the guiding assumption of the first set of essays when he asserts that the informing "I" behind autobiography is indispensable to any significance the genre could have. All of the final essays raise disconcerting questions about this assumption. Louis A. Renza writes about the " 'impersonating' effect of discourse" which unavoidably presses the first person of autobiography in the direction of a "de facto third-person pronoun."[7] Given the pressure exerted by language, which Renza calls "writing's law of gravity," the autobiographer has only two choices: either to give in to the pressure (as do Henry Adams and Norman Mailer when they make actual use of the third person for self-presentation), or openly to resist the pressure (as do many autobiographers from Rousseau to the present).

Michael Sprinker goes one step further in the last essay of the volume. Drawing on the work of Jacques Lacan, Michel Foucault, and Jacques Derrida, his essay joins autobiography to the ranks of *livres sans auteurs*. The struggle against writing's law of gravity is finally in vain, since "no autobiography can take place except within the boundaries of a writing where concepts of subject, self, and author collapse into the act of producing a text."[8] For Renza, the "self-writing" has trouble staying alive inside the text;

7. Renza, "The Veto of the Imagination," p. 279 (see note 6).
8. Sprinker, "Fictions of the Self," p. 342 (see note 6).

for Sprinker, the "self-written" cannot exist outside of it.

Elizabeth W. Bruss's questions about the autobiographical self arise within the context of film rather than texts. Unlike Renza and Sprinker, Bruss sees no necessary disenfranchisement of the self in the move from "life" to text. On the contrary, language offers, she says, a "peculiar fitness" for the expression, even the creation, of selfhood. Instead, Bruss anatomizes the transformation that takes place in the media shift from autobiographical text to autobiographical film. This move, and not the one from "life" to textual narrative, jeopardizes what she identifies as the "classical" autobiographical self by substituting an "eye" for the "I": the assumed unity of that "I" necessarily "decomposes" into the "almost exclusive elements of the person filmed (entirely visible; recorded and projected) and the person filming (entirely hidden; behind the camera eye)."[9]

Reflected in both sets of essays, though to varying degrees and certainly in quite different modes of discourse, are the assumptions of what Bruss identifies as "classical autobiography." The genre-assumptions of classical autobiography—more accurately, the assumptions of autobiography *theorists* about the genre—have largely to do with the self's position vis à vis itself and the world. The self knows itself, according to classical autobiography theory, from the inside out. That being the case, the self is the best, indeed, the only, source of self-knowledge. Gusdorf makes explicit this epistemology when he claims that "[n]o one can know better than I what I have thought, what I have wished."[10] Not only does the self know itself better than anyone else could; that knowledge necessarily remains a secret which can never be known by another: "Others, no matter how well intended, are forever going wrong; they describe the

9. Bruss, "Eye for I," p. 297 (see note 6).
10. Gusdorf, "Conditions and Limits of Autobiography," p. 35 (see note 3).

external figure, *the appearance they see and not the true person,* which always escapes them." In a word, the self's position on itself is a "privileged one."[11]

The ultimate expression of the self's privileged position is the Cartesian cogito. The price exacted for the self's access to itself is very high: nothing less than the world, from which the subject must remove itself in order to think. In the tradition of autobiography theory indirectly influenced by Descartes through Bergson, one finds this provisional act of unsituating the self from the world transformed into a condition of the self's authentic nature. Descartes' temporary removal has been petrified into a permanent feature of the autobiographical self when it is claimed by classical theorists that the "true" self is private and hidden behind its public version, which unavoidably masks or even distorts it (or, for Renza, presses it towards a de facto third person). The true self is not only private and hidden, they assume; it is also timeless and unchanging—here, again, in opposition to the public mask whose efforts at communication implicate it in the temporality of speaking. To avoid the contamination of time, the privacy of the true self must be made absolute. Any communication it has must be with itself, silent and timeless. Autobiography has therefore to be understood as a form of "transcendental voyeurism"—as though the reader were getting a second-hand account of what the self, watching and overhearing itself, has seen and heard.[12]

The genre-assumptions of classical autobiographical theory have influenced a long tradition of thought about the genre—from the watershed essay of Georges Gusdorf (who was himself influenced by the earlier work of Georg Misch and, through Misch, the even earlier historiography of Wil-

11. Ibid., p. 36. I will be arguing that the "true" self *is,* in fact, the appearing (or what I call the displayed) self. (*Italics mine.*)

12. The phrase is Elizabeth Bruss's on page 320.

helm Dilthey)[13] to the very recent application of a certain brand of phenomenology or of structuralism. Each, in its own way, deports autobiography from the country of vital experience to the desert island of Husserlian reduction or a reified textual system. At the center of these assumptions about autobiography is the hidden or ghostly self which is absolute, ineffable, and timeless. Being outside the momentum of temporality and beyond the reach of language, this self cannot be said to have a past at all: it never *was;* it simply *is.* It would be more accurate, then, to call this self the *anti*-autobiographical, not the autobiographical self.

Surely, there is good reason for the anxiety about the self which James Olney sees as motivating current interest in the genre of autobiography. More often than not, the self attributed to the genre is an *autos* which has been cut off from life, or the *bios* of autobiography. Given the starting point of most autobiography theory, the starting point of the private and hidden self writing from the inside out, it is not surprising to learn that autobiography reaches a dead end. The real question remains: was autobiography ever alive to begin with?

I intend the theory of autobiography put forward in these pages to be an answer, even an alternative, to classical autobiography theory. Rather than starting from the private act of a self writing, I begin from the cultural act of a self reading. Reading takes place at two moments of what I will be defining as the autobiographical situation: by the autobiographer who, in effect, is "reading" his or her life; and by the reader of the autobiographical text. This reading (or interpretive activity) takes place, moreover, by selves who

13. See Georg Misch, *A History of Autobiography in Antiquity,* trans. E. W. Dickes (Cambridge: Harvard University Press, 1951); and Wilhelm Dilthey, *Selected Writings of Wilhelm Dilthey,* selected, translated and introduced by H. P. Rickman (Cambridge: Cambridge University Press, 1976).

inhabit worlds, not by a subject who has had to pay the price of world-habitation for access to itself. The self who reads, whether it be the autobiographer or the reader of autobiography, is the *displayed self,* not the hidden self. The displayed self is the self who speaks, who lives in time, and, by virtue of living in time, who participates in depth and thus can experience the inter- and transpersonal grounds by which personal identity becomes possible. It is by means of language *(graphie)* that self both displays itself and has access to depth; it is also through language that self achieves and acknowledges its *bios.*

The self's impulse towards orientation in its world exhibits the *bios* of autobiography. Although the self already inhabits a world, its entry into the "perilous domain of history" makes it impossible simply to assume an unmediated relation to this world. At the same time, only because of self's already inhabiting the space-time of its world can autobiography take place. When the autobiographer brings a life "to language," he or she always adumbrates a perspective from somewhere—namely, from a world whose meanings and codes and even whose burden of unintelligibility serve to locate and ground that perspective. Autobiography does not defy the law of gravity which Louis Renza attributes to writing; instead, autobiography, in its orienting function, fulfills that law. In the very act of bringing life to language, the autobiographer discloses the ground that makes autobiography possible in the first place. The fact of the autobiographer's anchorage in the temporality (and spatiality) of his or her lived world constitutes the beginning as well as the *telos* of autobiography. Not as an escape from time, but as a plunge into it; not as a self's divestment of its world-involvement, but as an acknowledgment of its temporal experience as a vehicle of meaning—this is how autobiography displays its *bios.*

The self, then, displays, not distorts, itself by means of

language. Once *said,* however, the self always has (and "is") *more to be said* and even unsaid. In other words, the depth of the displayed self is not reduced to *mere* surface. Surface, in fact, can be a real clue, not merely a false scent, to what operates behind or beneath. As I will be arguing in later chapters, the relation of surface to depth in autobiographical narrative can best be understood as a synecdochical relation. Like metaphor, the trope of synecdoche stands for a part-whole relation. Unlike metaphor, however, which connotes an image in space, synecdoche suggests a quality in time. Only inside of time and displayed in the world can the self participate in depth. And only by rescuing the autobiographic genre from the essentialism of classical autobiography theory can it be restored to what Marjorie Grene has called the "category of life."[14]

While I have serious qualms about Georges Gusdorf's epistemological assumptions about autobiography, I think he is quite right in saying that the significance of autobiography lies not in its "literary function" but in its "anthropology."[15] This is not to say that the literary dimension of autobiography can be overlooked. It is rather to say that this dimension must be located and redefined within a more inclusive context—a context sufficiently capacious to account for autobiography as a human, cultural, and even a religious activity.

That we are, by and large, unable to think about autobiography in these larger terms is due in part to its critical neglect. But even more important is the failure on the part of the critical establishment to recognize and assess the reasons for its indifference and occasional animus toward what is, after all, a tradition of long standing in the history of letters.

14. See Marjorie Grene, *The Knower and the Known* (Berkeley: University of California Press, 1974).
15. Gusdorf, "Conditons and Limits of Autobiography," pp. 33–34.

The autobiographic genre having been absent from earlier thinking about the nature and function of literature, critics are now trying to fit autobiography into a procrustean bed that is unable to accommodate its distinctive contours. Recent literary criticism, in other words, tends to exert an unreconstructed hegemony over the autobiographic territory it has lately come to discover, conducting its business too much as usual and in seeming ignorance of the held-over assumptions which continue to inform its *modus operandi.*

Such, at least, is the case in the operation of aesthetic assumptions whose late nineteenth- and early twentieth-century reification of certain structural features (harmony, balance between the inner and the outer, wholeness) was instituted in isolation from the different considerations the unruly behavior of autobiography would have demanded. Rather than calling into question the adequacy of these assumptions in the face of new literary evidence, many critics have turned instead to taxonomical strategies of ordering the autobiographic genre into its sub-species (memoir, diary, confession, portrait, and so on) in the attempt to control rather than to respond to its strangeness.[16] In the case of certain structuralist approaches to autobiography, the ranks have been closed altogether against the incursion of any nonscriptable feature of textuality outside the fail-safe linguistic system of binary oppositions.

I want to address this overall problem of conceptualization by thinking about the genre-questions of autobiography in the larger context of hermeneutics, narrative theory, and the current debate about the determinate meaning of texts.

16. I have in mind the early classifying work of Roy Pascal, *Design and Truth in Autobiography* (Cambridge: Harvard University Press, 1960); and, more recently, William L. Howarth, "Some Principles of Autobiography," *New Literary History* V (1974):363–81. Helpful as these studies are, they fail to address the *first* questions of autobiography, which are questions of an anthropological, not a literary, nature.

Such questions, in order that they recover for autobiography its human and cultural significance, must themselves be situated in the "world" that readers inhabit—a world, in other words, of contingent historical experience. To locate the critical task in such a world is, to be sure, to relinquish hold on the clear and certain knowledge of determinate meanings. At the same time, such a relocation allows cancellation of that "insurance against doubt" which the late French phenomenologist, M. Merleau-Ponty, ascribed to the Cartesian cogito, an insurance policy "whose premiums are more onerous than the loss for which it is to indemnify us: for it is to . . . move to a type of certitude that will never restore to us the 'there is' of the world."[17] What can be gained in place of world-less certitude are the richer terms of *depth* and *significance*, problematic and provisional though they be, that can restore autobiography to the category of life.

What allows reinstatement of autobiography to the country of vital experience is the reconceptualization made possible by what I am calling the autobiographical situation. A hermeneutics of restoration, the autobiographical situation makes way for thinking about autobiography from three different angles, or in terms of three interrelated moments. Each of these angles or moments offers a nonreductive way into the phenomenon of autobiographical activity. Each rests on and assumes the others.

Constituting the autobiographical situation are the autobiographical impulse, the autobiographical perspective, and the autobiographical response. The *impulse* arises out of the effort to confront the problem of temporality and can be assumed operative in *any* attempt to make sense of experience. The *perspective* shapes autobiographical impulse by

17. M. Merleau-Ponty, *The Visible and the Invisible*, ed. Claude Lefort, trans. Alphonso Lingis (Evanston: Northwestern University Press, 1968), pp. 36–37.

bringing it to language and displaying it as narrative surface; it is informed by problems of locating and gaining access to the past. The *response* has to do with the problem of appropriation and the reader's relation to the autobiographical text. All of these moments (or angles) are levels of interpretation and part of a world characterized by finitude and historicity. Only within such a world can understanding take place. As the principal mode of experiencing the world, finitude and temporality do not stand in the way of our understanding but make way for it.[18]

The autobiographical impulse exhibits the most basic level at which we live as human agents, in a certain situation and always in relation to certain assumed meanings which we know as culture. As a dimension of depth or latency, this level has been addressed in a variety of ways by those whose interests, broadly speaking, are phenomenological. I have in mind what Michael Polanyi calls the "tacit dimension" or the more-than-we-can-say of what we know; what Merleau-Ponty calls the "anchorage" of the "already there"; what Gaston Bachelard refers to as the "cradle of the house"; and what José Ortega y Gasset means by *"creencia"*—that "zone of stability" which has to do with the ideas we are, not the ideas we have.[19]

18. The world of finitude and historicity within which autobiography must be situated is what Hans-Georg Gadamer calls the "hermeneutical universe." For much of my thinking about the problem of autobiography, I am indebted to Gadamer's work. See especially, *Truth and Method*, translation edited by Garret Barden and John Cumming (New York: The Seabury Press, 1975).

19. See Michael Polanyi, *The Tacit Dimension* (Garden City, N. Y.: Doubleday & Co., 1966); M. Merleau-Ponty, *Phenomenology of Perception*, trans. Colin Smith (London: Routledge & Kegan Paul, 1962); Gaston Bachelard, *The Poetics of Space*, trans. Maria Jolas (New York: Orion Press, 1964); and José Ortega y Gasset, "History as a System," in *History as a System and Other Essays Toward a Philosophy of History* (New York: W. W. Norton & Co., 1961).

Never is it entirely possible to make explicit this level of lived depth, since any act of knowing rests itself on unstated dimensions. Ortega illustrates the behavior of latency when he meditates on the old adage about not seeing the forest for the trees.[20] This is so, he argues, because it is necessarily the case. Were the forest to be seen, it would no longer be the forest but a bank of trees. The forest always lies beyond our ken, somewhere behind the trees, because it exists *as* latency.

It is likewise the case that autobiography can never exhume all of that buried life making up the past. But just because all of the past cannot be *present*ed does not mean that it is therefore absent from the autobiographical text. Such would be the case only if time (both "real" time and "narrative" time) were experienced as a series of nows, all of them strung on a single line. Time, however, is experienced more like the thickness of a palimpsest, as Marcel Proust knew so well—like a parchment on which layers of writing have been superimposed. Just because something is not fully visible does not mean its presence cannot be experienced. The past provides fullness to the present as both a push and pull behind its surface. In our ordinary "perceptual faith," we easily know the presence of the unpresented.[21] We know, for instance, that objects have insides as well as outsides, backs as well as fronts. We know, too, that people have pasts (and even futures) as well as presents. In the "Tintern Abbey" poem I will be analyzing in a later chapter, the figure of Dorothy functions as an instrument of perceptual faith for the poet. While Wordsworth is unable to "paint" (to make fully visible) his own past, he can experience its presence in the interhuman community provided by his

20. See José Ortega y Gasset, *Meditations on Quixote,* trans. Evelyn Rugg and Diego Marin (New York: W. W. Norton & Co., 1961), pp. 59–60.

21. The phrase is Merleau-Ponty's.

sister. Only for a self cut off from a world does there exist no middle term between the present and the absent.

The fact that the past can never be made fully explicit is no deterrent to autobiography. On the contrary, the very indeterminateness or opacity that characterizes our relations with the past enjoins and supports the act of autobiography —not as an invasion of depth, but as testimony to its enlivening presence. Autobiographical impulse, then, operates as a pre-textual level which grounds both perspective and response. Its latency comes to enactment in the move from life to text. As Thoreau discovers, the "bottom"—toward which his autobiographical excursion "wedges"—finally displays itself in the coming of spring. What lies at bottom is waiting to surface in the act of attention.

By means of the angle that autobiographical impulse affords, we can say something about the display of groundedness: how it is that language displays the depth of lived experience without defying any law of gravity. But it is only at the second moment of the autobiographical situation, the textual moment of perspective, that we can angle in on the groundedness of display, or how it is that the autobiographical self always comes *from* somewhere.

The adumbration of perspective constitutes the move to the second level of autobiography, the level at which autobiographical impulse becomes autobiographical perspective. This second level is the level of textuality wherein the assumed meanings of lived depth—Ortega's *creencias*— are shaped and interpreted by means of language. This level of interpretive activity is operative in all efforts toward second-order knowledge or the attempt to "discover" the structure of meaning in any experience. Whatever its modality—scientific, historical, poetic, or otherwise—this structure of meaning cannot be said to exist independent of interpretation, although the most compelling structures are assumed to be "there," in the nature of things. At this second level, however, such meanings are always shaped, and the shaping has to do with the *placing* of the interpreter. But just as there is no structure of meaning inherent in the nature of things, there is no act of interpretation that can be understood simply as the projection of a disembodied consciousness outside of time and space. When Robert Frost said that "there ought to be in everything you write some sign that you come from almost anywhere," he might more accurately have claimed that there is, in fact, *always* such a sign.[22]

Autobiography, at the level of perspective, involves a certain mode of self-placing in relation to the autobiographer's past and from a particular standpoint in his or her present. As Karl J. Weintraub has noted, the standpoint of autobiography occupies "a point in time . . . located on the lifeline of the writer somewhere beyond a moment of crisis. . . ."[23] Robert Frost's "anywhere," from which the autobiographer comes, is more than a geographical place or even the space-time of a particular historical setting. While such information is usually provided or implied in the account, the autobiographer does more than issue a report on where he or she has been and what he or she has done. Autobiography, as one critic has rightly stated, is not merely a matter of "copying oneself down."[24]

The autobiographical perspective has rather to do with taking oneself up and bringing oneself to language. Furthermore, the language of autobiography (the language that, at this second level of textuality, *is* autobiography) is not to be

22. Robert Frost, at Bread Loaf, 1958, quoted by Richard Poirier, *Robert Frost: The Work of Knowing* (New York: Oxford University Press, 1977), p. ix.
23. Karl J. Weintraub, "Autobiography and Historical Consciousness," *Critical Inquiry* I (1975): 824.
24. Shapiro, "The Dark Continent of Literature," p. 421.

taken as a third-person account of a life that just happens to be one's own—an objective entity, complete in itself, and existing in a world of other objects. The autobiographical act of taking up one's life in language is not, in other words, an accounting after the fact, as though the telling were a memorandum on what has already taken place.

Autobiography is a presencing, in Augustine's words, of "man in his deep." What is made present is not merely a past that is past. What is presenced is a reality, always new, to which the past has contributed but which stands, as it were, in front of the autobiographer. To lay claim to one's life, and thereby to become "fierce with reality," is to understand that reality as something to which one is continually trying to catch up but which one can never outstrip.[25] Were it possible to catch up, if the "spatio-temporal horizons could, even theoretically, be made explicit," then "nothing could exist; I should hover above the world, so that all times and places, far from becoming simultaneously real, would become unreal, because I should live in none of them and would be involved nowhere."[26]

The taking up of one's life in language that adumbrates the autobiographical perspective testifies to the autobiographer's particular involvement in the world, a landing rather than a hovering. The finitude of that involvement, the fact that one exists somewhere and not everywhere, constitutes one's access to the past: "If I am at all times and everywhere, then I am at no time and nowhere."[27] Perspective can never fill out or complete the canvas of one's experience, because that canvas is always moving and changing. To avoid its becoming a form of squatter's rights, the placement involved

25. Florida Scott-Maxwell, *The Measure of My Days* (New York: Alfred A. Knopf, 1975), p. 42.
26. Merleau-Ponty, *Phenomenology of Perception*, p. 332.
27. Ibid.

in adumbrating autobiographical perspective must be par-ticipled. And just as placement must be understood as *placing,* an ongoing rather than a settled process, the autobio-graphical effort at possessing one's life must be understood as a movement toward possibility as much as a turning around to the already achieved. If one is to become "fierce with reality," as my epigraph puts it, then it is toward the future that the act of autobiography heuristically points. It is in the future that reality stands waiting to be *real*ized; it is from the future that time comes.

What the angle of autobiographical perspective dis-closes is not only the placing or "fromness" that grounds self's display; this angle allows us to appreciate the dimen-sion of futurity in the depth of lived experience. Autobiogra-phy's arc of meaning projects forward where that meaning can be realized.

The forward movement of autobiography leads to the third moment of the autobiographical situation: the autobio-graphical response of the reader. The activity of reading as an indispensable part of the production of textual meaning has, until recently, been taken for granted, even among those critics who otherwise had insisted on the autonomy of texts. The so-called text itself of the formalists had, after all, to be *read* in order that its equilibrium be tested, its unity uncovered. Since the affective level of literary works has been reinstated as a legitimate consideration in criticism, the reading act has come into new prominence. "Affective sty-listics," the "dynamics of literary response," the "implied reader," and in some quarters the inevitability of "misread-ing"—all of this has become ordinary coinage in the market-place of literary criticism.[28]

28. See Stanley Fish, "Literature in the Reader: Affective Stylis-tics," *New Literary History* II (1970): 123–62; Norman Holland, *The Dy-namics of Literary Response* (New York: Oxford University Press, 1968);

All too often, this newly discovered dimension of textual experience—or the rediscovery of what surely goes back as far as Longinus—has led to the psychologizing of literature or to the professionalization of reading. In the case of the former, the text becomes a behavioristic model to which response can be quantified, measured, and even predicted. In the case of the latter, the reader must don special attire either to plunge for deep structures or to catapult out of time in order to reconstruct authorial intention or to anatomize originating genres.

But the autobiographical response, like the autobiographical self, cannot be quarantined to some sterile corner outside of culture. It belongs instead to the larger cultural context where reading is simply part of a capacity to function adequately as a human being. In modern western culture (the culture out of which autobiography emerged), literacy is indispensable to fully human survival.

Reading takes place, then, in a cultural context—a context whose symbols and whose "webs of significance" are both products of and models for such interpretive activity as reading represents. It is out of this context, and by virtue of it, that readers respond. As I hope to show in a later chapter, that response combines two modes of interpretive activity. On the one hand, the reader experiences the autobiographical text as an occasion of discovery: of seeing in the text the heretofore unexpressed or unrecognized depth of the reader's self—not as a mirror image, nor even as a particular manifestation of some shared idea of selfhood, but as an instance of interpretive activity that *risks* display. What the reader finds displayed is that vulnerability which makes it possible to celebrate the finitude of his or her own selving. In a word, the reader discovers the *possibility* of selfhood

---

and Harold Bloom, *The Map of Misreading* (New York: Oxford University Press, 1975).

through interpretation. This, then, is *what* the reader is enabled to see by means of what Proust calls the "optical instrument" of the text.

In addition to what is seen and discovered, there is also the matter of *how* the instrument of the text enables the reader to see. While the first mode of experiencing the text might be called participatory, this second mode exemplifies the "distantiating" function of reading which enables the reader to look at the universe of common experience from a perspective different from his or her own.[29] As is the case in all serious literature, the autobiographical text puts the reader to work—both on it and on himself or herself in the effort to become the reader the text demands. In so becoming that reader, customary habits of response are necessarily violated. The reader experiences the *otherness* of the text which keeps the appropriative activity of interpretation from becoming expropriative. The autobiographical response includes both kinds of activity—the interpretive modes of hermeneutics and of poetics—and brings them into the new relation of what I will be calling the "stereoscope of readership."

This third moment of response serves as the angle of initial entry into the autobiographical situation. Since it is located on the other "sides" of both the autobiographical impulse (the self's depth-disposition towards orientation in its world) and the autobiographical perspective (the display of lived depth at the level of narrative surface), autobiographical response occupies that point of vantage—in front of both, as it were—from which the relation of depth and surface can be realized. Because it is only from this position

29. For the notions of "participation" and "distantiation" I am indebted to the work of Paul Ricoeur. See especially *Interpretation Theory: Discourse and the Surplus of Meaning* (Fort Worth: The Texas Christian University Press, 1976).

that the stereoscopic relation can be activated, the moment
of autobiographical response serves additionally as the presenting moment of the genre; it is in the "virtual space"
between the text and the reader[30]—the space where their
respective horizons may fuse—that new understanding can
take place. New understanding allows neither assimilation
(the reader's takeover of the text) nor accommodation (the
text's takeover of the reader). Autobiographical response requires, instead, an integration—what Hans-Georg Gadamer
calls a "fusion of horizons"—that acknowledges and makes
productive use of the tension between the text and the
reader, as well as of their common participation in the temporal dimension of depth and their joint membership in the
category of life.

Genre, I am arguing, is first of all an instrument of
reading, not primarily a formula for writing. As such, genre
is what enables the reader to locate himself or herself before
the text and thereby to have access to the possible meaning
of the text. Genre provides what one critic calls a "space for
qualitative response,"[31] what I would call a theater for displaying ourselves to one another. Further, I use the term
reader to identify a position, not a person. The agent one
normally regards as the writer can also occupy the position
of the reader, as I want to demonstrate when I use Proust's
"Marcel" to illustrate the autobiographical response in
Chapter 4. In addition to being (at various times and, at the
end, simultaneously) the main character, the narrator, and
the author of the book, Marcel is also a reader of his book-

---

30. The notion of "virtual space" between the text and the reader
is Wolfgang Iser's in *The Implied Reader: Patterns of Communication in
Prose Fiction from Bunyan to Beckett* (Baltimore: The Johns Hopkins
Press, 1974).

31. See Charles Altieri, "The Qualities of Action: Part II, *Boundary
2 V* (1977): 899.

like life. Only when he discovers his role as reader does he realize his vocation as author. He has this realization at the end of the novel *we* are about to finish reading, but Marcel is about to begin writing. He will write the book from the outside in, not inside out—in other words, from the position on the *other* side of his lived past which the reader-self occupies. He has access to this other side—the side, as it were, in *front* of his life—through the eyes of the aging friends around him at the afternoon party of the Guermantes. The reflection he sees in these eyes provides him with what he acknowledges as "the first truthful mirror I had ever encountered."[32] In starting from the appearing self that others see, he can more surely and truthfully move back to who he is. To set out from the self's own shadowy interior, however, is to remain forever in the dark with only the certitude of one's private sensations. Only by moving out from the intersubjective world *where one already is* can one reach the destination of selfhood: from *bios* to *autos;* from *autos,* however, to solipsism.

As the reader of his or her life, the autobiographer inhabits the hermeneutic universe where all understanding takes place. The autobiographer serves, by this habitation, as the paradigmatic reader; and the autobiographical text, embodying this reading, becomes, in turn, a model of the possibilities and problems of all interpretive activity. Defining the conditions and limits of autobiography, this hermeneutic universe provides the context I have been calling the autobiographical situation. When relocated in this context, the autobiographical self, aesthetically deadened by classical au-

32. Marcel Proust, *Remembrance of Things Past,* trans. C. K. Scott Moncrieff and Andreas Mayor (New York: Random House, 1970), Vol. II., p. 1046. Subsequent citations will come from this as well as the first volume of this edition and will be indicated by page numbers following the quoted matter.

tobiography theory which abstracts it from its lived situation, can return to the category of life.

The self that comes to life is not, however, the self which, like Narcissus, grasped for its mirror-image and drowned in certainty; rather it is the self which, like Antaeus, has its life in groundedness. As long as this mythical giant remained in contact with earth, his mother, he remained invincible. Antaeus was finally killed by Hercules who, learning his secret, suspended him in the air. As an act of orientation by means of which the self inhabits and not merely projects a possible world of significance, autobiography embodies the story of Antaeus and not, as so many are ready to assume, the story of Narcissus. Understood as the story of Antaeus, the real question of the autobiographical self then becomes *where do I belong?* not, who am I? The question of the self's identity becomes a question of the self's location in a world.[33]

In the chapters that follow, I will be using a variety of texts to illustrate the locative activity inherent in the autobiographical situation. Four of these texts—*Walden*, the two Wordsworth poems ("Resolution and Independence" and "Tintern Abbey"), and *Remembrance of Things Past*—are firmly established in the literary canon but, by and large, they have not been seriously considered as autobiography. Augustine's *Confessions*, on the other hand, has secure membership in the autobiographical tradition (for some wrong reasons, as I shall argue), but has been little regarded as literature. Different from both the *Confes-*

33. A primary feature of true autobiography, I will be arguing in Chapter 5, is its "worldliness," a concept I borrow from Hannah Arendt. For a helpful analysis of Arendt's notion of worldliness, see George Kateb, "Freedom and Worldliness in the Thought of Hannah Arendt," *Political Theory* V (1977): 141–82.

sions and the works I use from "high" literary culture, *Black Elk Speaks*, though a cult-book for a number of years, has only recently been admitted into the literary canon, this recognition having come by way of the spotlight on autobiography in literary circles.[34] *Black Elk Speaks* is both a more recent and, at the same time, a more traditional piece of writing than any of the literary texts I use. More memoiristic than the others, it is a tribal narrative orally recounted in the 1930s by an old Oglala Sioux medicine man to the poet-anthropologist John Neihardt. As an "as told to" (or in a later emendation, an "as told *through*") example of autobiographical writing, this text raises special questions which I will be addressing.

I will be using (and I trust not abusing) these texts as occasions for reflecting on and fleshing out the three angles or moments of the autobiographical situation as well as for defining the religious hermeneutic of Augustine's *credo ut intelligam* as the "worldly" context of true autobiography. Although I will be addressing these moments and features one by one, there will be inevitable overlapping and even some repetition in my respective discussions. Not only are these moments and features themselves interrelated within the autobiographical situation; any of the texts I use for the purpose of illustrating one of these aspects could just as well be used to illustrate the others. True autobiography—and this is the basis of its truth—is simultaneously characterized by impulse, perspective, and response, as well as by the hermeneutic of *credo ut intelligam* and the features of what Hannah Arendt calls "worldliness."[35]

34. One of the first, and certainly the most important, literary critics to recognize the merits of *Black Elk Speaks* as literature and autobiography is Robert Sayre. See his essay, "Vision and Experience in *Black Elk Speaks*," *College English* XXXII (1971): 509–35.

35. In addition, the analysis being presented is, after all, being conducted by one person, myself, who already knows what can be seen on the "other" side of something, even as she is focussing on "this" side.

Rather than "giving" these texts to my reader, then, I will be "taking them on," to use Barbara Herrnstein Smith's distinction.[36] When looked at in the new hermeneutical context of the autobiographical situation, these texts "oblige" me to supply them with meanings. Along with Professor Smith, I hasten to add that this obligation gives no license for "daydreaming." As she argues, their "value lies not simply in provoking [reflection] . . . but also in shaping and, indeed, resisting it."[37]

Like texts that resist as well as provoke interpretation, the lived past, too, resists total interpretive possession, as I said in my earlier discussion of autobiographical perspective. Autobiography completes no pictures. Instead, it rejects wholeness or harmony, ascribed by formalists to the well-made art object, as a false unity which serves as no more than a defense against the self's deeper knowledge of its finitude. Finitude, as it turns out, is the self's only defense against the false unity that would remove it from the temporal dimension of depth. Finitude operates as a correctability factor against that all-encompassing schema which can promise invulnerability but only at the price of the self's real life. The primary example of such a schema—or what might be called ideology—is, of course, the classical autobiographical self which wins eternity but loses the possibility of meaning that resides only in time.

When I define autobiography as a poetics of experience, I want to call attention to this process of "schema and correction" which not only characterizes experience but

---

Though I proceed in the manner of a *bricoleur*, not a systematician, I nonetheless cannot pretend to be totally ignorant of what comes before and after what I am doing at any one time.

36. Barbara Herrnstein Smith, *On the Margins of Discourse: The Relation of Literature to Language* (Chicago: University of Chicago Press, 1978), p. 146.

37. Ibid., p. 145.

makes it available to us *as our own*. [38] Only when our assumptions about "the ways things are" are tested and corrected, rather than simply corroborated, do we become aware of having these assumptions in the first place. And only when the "fit" between old schema and new events is missing can these new events come into our field of attention. Otherwise, they pass unnoticed and therefore unexperienced. Although I apply this model of experience in any explicit way only to Wordsworth's poems (as the correction that the experience of "landscape" enjoins on the prior schema of the "picturesque"), it is operative in the other texts as well: in *Walden* as the move from deliberation to "dehiscence"; in *Remembrance of Things Past* as the move from what Roger Shattack calls the "esthetic of the false scent" to the "esthetic of the double take";[39] in the *Confessions* as the antidote of circumstantial "place" which rescues Augustine from the vagrancy of his search for final answers; and in *Black Elk Speaks* as the revisioning performance of the autobiographical act itself which must take the place of the broken schema of the Indian nation's "hoop."

Experience includes more than the sensations of touch, smell, taste, sight, and hearing. Were experience restricted to these sensations, it would be the strictly private affair that Gerard Manley Hopkins identifies as his own singular self: "that taste of myself, of *I* and *me* above and in all things, which is more distinctive than the taste of ale or alum, more distinctive than the smell of walnutleaf or camphor."[40] But even to *identify* these experiences as the experience of the self and not as random floating particles which belong to no

38. See further discussion of these ideas on pages 69–71.
39. Roger Shattuck, *Proust's Binoculars: A Study of Memory, Time, and Recognition in A la recherche du temps perdu* (New York: Random House, 1963).
40. Quoted by Olney, *Autobiography: Essays Theoretical and Critical*, p. 23.

one or nothing in particular requires a "sixth sense," as Hannah Arendt calls it, which connects and locates the other five in a context. This is the sense she calls the "common sense" or *sensus communis* whose function it is to "[fit] the sensations of my strictly private five senses—so private that sensations in their mere sensational quality and intensity are incommunicable—into a common world shared by others."[41] The *sensus communis* supplies a threefold commonness which, in fact, guarantees reality. This sixth sense makes it possible, first of all, to identify as single and the same an object which I can smell, touch, see, and taste. An apple, for example, is not four distinct things—the thing-I-smell, the thing-I-touch, the thing-I-see, and the thing-I-taste. Moreover, the apple that appears to me simultaneously in these four ways is also the apple that appears to others from their point of vantage—that is, as an "it-seems-to-me." "The subjectivity of the it-seems-to-me is remedied," Arendt says, "by the fact that the same object also appears to others though its mode of appearance may be different."[42] Finally, the unity of the five senses and the "sharability" of the experienced object both take place in a common world —a network of tacit relationships and allegiances, of unspoken assumptions and expectations, a repertory of convictions and of "webs of significance" which we call culture.[43]

The common world of culture which shapes and is shaped by experience is, finally, a fiduciary context within which one's sensation of reality arises out of the trust one

41. Hannah Arendt, *The Life of the Mind: Thinking* (New York: Harcourt Brace Jovanovich, 1978), p. 50.

42. Ibid.

43. See Clifford Geertz, *The Interpretation of Cultures* (New York: Basic Books, 1963), p. 5. Geertz writes: "The concept of culture I espouse . . . is essentially a semiotic one. Believing, with Max Weber, that man is an animal suspended in webs of significance he himself has spun, I take culture to be those webs, and the analysis of it to be therefore not an experimental science in search of law but an interpretive one in search of meaning."

can have in and within this world. As a poetics of experience, autobiography is a human, cultural, and religious act taking place within this context of trust or what Michael Polanyi calls the "system of acceptances" which grounds all of our knowledge, even—and most especially—the knowledge we have of ourselves.[44]

Its fiduciary grounding enables autobiography to resist one final thing—the temptation to despair so compelling in a world of loss and of the "weightlessness" Nietzsche ascribed to the modern breakdown of the *sensus communis*.[45] The tacit commitment of trust to a world that guarantees our very sense of who we are reveals its obverse side in this final resistance—namely, in a certain kind of refusal which Merleau-Ponty compares with the phenomenon of the "phantom limb." The amputee continues to experience the "presence" of the limb which has been removed, neither as a result of self-delusion nor as a result of a conscious decision to ignore a painful experience. The phantom limb results instead from the self's *prior* commitment "to a certain physical and inter-human world" and its continuing "to tend toward [that] world despite handicaps and amputations. . . ."[46] In light of this fundamental gesture of resistance to mutilation that autobiography displays—to the mutilation of *temps perdu* every bit as much as to the mutilation of *jambe perdu*, the genre could be classified in one of two ways: as a form of survival-literature or as a form of comedy. In either case, the self is brought to size even as it is mortalized.

44. Michael Polanyi, *Personal Knowledge: Towards a Post-Critical Philosophy* (Chicago: University of Chicago Press, 1974), p. 267. Our grounding in such a context is what frees us from "objectivism": "to realize that we can voice our ultimate convictions only from within our convictions—from within the whole system of acceptances that are logically prior to any particular assertion of our own, prior to the holding of any particular piece of knowledge"—this realization, for Polanyi, liberates us.
45. See a further discussion of these ideas on pages 35–36.
46. Merleau-Ponty, *Phenomenology of Perception*, p. 81.

2

The Autobiographical Impulse

WALDEN AND THE TEMPORAL MODE
OF AUTOBIOGRAPHICAL NARRATIVE

> The earth is not a mere fragment of dead
> history, stratum upon stratum like the leaves of
> a book, to be studied by geologists and
> antiquaries chiefly, but living poetry like the
> leaves of the trees, which precede flowers and
> fruits,—not a fossil earth, but a living earth.
> —Henry David Thoreau, *Walden*

Until the day before yesterday, autobiography was looked on, if noticed at all, as "the dark continent of literature."[1] Its territory is under intense exploration today, much of it seemingly colonized and carved up into more easily managed sub-divisions like the diary, the memoir, the confession, or the literary self-portrait. Earlier a victim of benign neglect, autobiography seems now a victim of the taxonomical imperative—an imperative that serves more often to control the autobiographic genre than to understand its unruly behavior.

So firm a standing does the genre currently enjoy that it is even being deconstructed. No sooner has autobiography been certified a *bona fide* genre and worthy, therefore, of serious literary attention, than it is now declared a hoax, or

---

1. Stephen A. Shapiro, "The Dark Continent of Literature: Autobiography," Comparative Literature Studies V (1968): 421–54.

defined as a mausoleum preserving a "self" which otherwise would not exist at all. As for its mirage-like status, autobiography is viewed as but an illusory appearance of selfhood which masks the reality of a True Self that exists elsewhere. As one critic has recently put it, the "I" of autobiography is simply a " 'dummy' ego"—a kind of Charlie McCarthy whose voice and movement are produced from some other location.[2] Autobiography, according to this argument, can be no more than a failed version of the autobiographer's real self, which is presumed buried under its various and changing appearances and therefore ineffable. The self cannot be put into words since, in Hemingway parlance, to say it is to lose it. Or in the terms I will be using, to convert the lived past into the presentness of language, is, according to this view, to sacrifice *depth* to mere *surface*.

The other view of autobiography rests on a very different set of assumptions.[3] While the crypto-Platonists argue that language distorts and trivializes the self, the anti-metaphysicians deny the self any status whatsoever outside of language. Despite their differing assumptions about the relation of self and language, both views place on autobiography a "demand of total explicitness" which refuses any middle ground between presence and absence, allowing no place for the "lurking opacity behind what can be clearly formulated."[4] What this demand requires is not that the autobiographer *qua* Rousseau tell all, but that the remembered past and the anticipated future be superintended by an absolute present: in other words, that the life that has been and is even

2. See Louis A. Renza, "The Veto of the Imagination: A Theory of Autobiography" in James Olney, ed., *Autobiography: Essays Theoretical and Critical* (Princeton: Princeton University Press, 1980).

3. See, for example, Jeffrey Mehlman, *A Structural Study of Autobiography: Proust, Leiris, Sartre, Lévi-Strauss* (Ithaca: Cornell University Press, 1974).

4. Marjorie Grene, *The Knower and the Known* (Berkeley: University of California Press, 1974), p. 157.

now being lived (in the act of writing it) be presented, as it were, on a single line, timeless yet immediate.

Neither view leaves room for what I take to be the human, and even religious, significance of autobiography, since both cut out of it the very heart of its generic achievement: namely, the extent to which autobiography, more than any other form of narrative, takes up the problem of depth—not by raising depth to an absolute present where it would become mere surface, but by enacting the reciprocity between depth and surface in what constitutes a cultural act of reading the self, rather than a private act of writing the self. The reading of oneself is always a cultural reading since self-knowledge, far from being transcendent or free-floating, is always grounded in the signs of one's existence that are received from others, as well as from the works of culture by which one is interpreted. Such views as I have mentioned —the one that assumes autobiography to be a private act of the self writing, the other that assumes autobiography to be part of a reified textual system—overlook the cultural dimension of the autobiographical act. They take into account neither the reading self of the autobiographer nor the reader we necessarily become when we set out to understand the autobiographical text. Henry David Thoreau became such a reader, a "faithful reader," as he named the activity. He became not only a faithful reader of Nature but, as I want to show, a faithful reader of the self.

In starting with the autobiographical impulse, I would seem to be reversing my argument about the presenting moment of the autobiographical situation since, as I defined it in the previous chapter, this impulse operates at a pre-textual level in the latent dimension of depth. Nonetheless I begin with this level, not as the first point of entry into the genre of autobiography, but in view of the fact that this level anchors the other two: depth is the level of proto-interpretation from which autobiographical perspective is adumbrated, as well as the level from which the reader responds.

Throughout this chapter and the next, I will be conducting my respective analyses of *Walden* and Wordsworth's poetry at the third level of autobiographical response, but, to use Michael Polanyi's useful distinction, I will be attending *from* this level and not *to* it. In this chapter I will be focusing my attention on two interpretive issues which, in my view, serve to disclose the character of depth. These issues have to do with the relation between autobiography and the life of the autobiographer and the function of language in revealing the depth of that life.

While the relation between autobiography and the life of the autobiographer has to do with locating and gaining access to the past, problems to which I will be turning in my next chapter on autobiographical perspective, the text-life relation at the level of autobiographical impulse is a *narrative issue*. If the move from the tacit level of life to the manifest level of text is a move that is creative and not destructive of the self, if, in other words, narrative display is not an invasion of depth, there are several claims to be made about the nature and function of narrative itself: (1) that there is a fittingness between the narrative mode of story and the depth experience of living in time; (2) that the strategy of narration is such that the writing of one's life story preserves and even enhances the depth-dimension of temporality and that, therefore, this strategy does not presume that everything can be stretched out, as it were, on a single line of narrative surface. Narrative surface, in other words, is not *mere* surface; (3) that these first two claims rest on yet a third, namely, that narrative represents an essentially temporal mode and, further, that autobiography as the bringing of one's life to language is possible because of that fact and not in spite of it. Autobiography fulfills, not defies, writing's law of gravity.

One basis for the fittingness between narrative and life lies in the eidetic compulsion for wholes that has been a commonplace of narrative theory since Aristotle's *Poetics.* Whether that whole is textually constituted, as for Aristotle, or whether it is based, as for certain recent critics,[5] on the "before" and "after" that makes for the formal quality of experience itself, this compulsion is part and parcel of all our sense-making activity as human beings. We tell stories, participate in rituals, or write history in order to achieve those "concords" which alone enable us to comprehend our experience in the world and to discover its significance.[6]

Such sense-making activity, basic to both narrative and life, involves as much a "making" as a "finding." There is no avoiding what Schleiermacher identified as the "hermeneutical circle," that mutual shaping of parts and imagined whole which characterizes all of our efforts at understanding. It is simply a question of where we enter that circle and the degree of critical reflection we bring to our own interpretive performance. This performance (in the case, for example, of historical narrative) entails the decision about what data should be excluded from any particular explanatory account, as well as the even more basic decision about what, in the first place, constitutes the data for selection. This matter of selection is as unavoidable for the computer

5. See, for example, Stephen Crites, "The Narrative Quality of Experience," *Journal of the American Academy of Religion* (1971): 291–311; and Barbara Hardy, *Tellers and Listeners: The Narrative Imagination* (London: The Athlone Press, 1975).

6. The idea of *concord* comes from Frank Kermode, *The Sense of an Ending: Studies in the Theory of Fiction* (New York: Oxford University Press, 1967).

historian of today as it was for the nineteenth-century theorist who, like Hegel and Nietzsche, rejected outright the Rankean belief in the "innocent eye."

Nonetheless historians and literary critics alike have recently called into question the possibility of any longer telling the "story" of the past.[7] Given the multiplicity of evidence now available to the modern historian, along with the narrative presumption that "life is susceptible of comprehension and thus of management," both history and the novel, it is argued, must inevitably be "betrayed into simplicity" if they are presented as story.[8] A critic of historiography like Claude Lévi-Strauss would go even further. Arguing that historical accounts are *"nothing but* interpretations," Lévi-Strauss sees these accounts as the historian's imposition of a "fraudulent outline" on the so-called data.[9]

Without going to such lengths, it is possible, however, to raise some serious questions about the efficacy of the built-in desire for comprehensiveness that characterizes much of the literature and history writing of the nineteenth and early twentieth centuries. Both of them may be said to participate in what Warner Berthoff calls "the romance of order" which tries to prove "the courage-establishing hypothesis" that the world is "controllable."[10] When the desire for control is uppermost, both literature and history can be turned into implements of ideology, a "paradigmatic rigid-

7. For this section of my discussion, I am indebted to Lionel Trilling's discussion of the narrative past in *Sincerity and Authenticity* (Cambridge: Harvard University Press, 1972). In what follows I have made use of portions of my essay, "Autobiography and the Narrative Experience of Temporality as Depth," *Soundings* LX (1977): 194–209.

8. Trilling, p. 135.

9. Haydon White, "Interpretation in History," in *Tropics of Discourse: Essays in Cultural Criticism* (Baltimore: The Johns Hopkins University Press, 1978), p. 55.

10. Warner Berthoff, *Fiction and Events: Essays in Criticism and Literary History* (New York: E. P. Dutton & Co, 1971), p. 42.

ity" which, in its most extreme form, can contribute—and, in the view of some, *has* contributed—to totalitarianism.[11] Such a use of narrative, in either its literary or historical forms, is, of course, a misuse, and J. H. Plumb's *The Death of the Past* is correct in pointing out how the story of the past has all too often been exploited in order to sanction such abuses as racial oppression in the present.[12]

But to pronounce the *death* of the past, as Plumb's title does, is to overlook the positive use to which narrative can be put, not alone as a *finding* of certain facts, as though these facts are apodictically present, but as a *making* which, together with finding, recognizes the heuristic function of all narrative. Such an understanding of narrative as discovery *and* creation fulfills the "recurring need," as Frank Kermode has put it, "for adjustment in the interest of reality as well as control."[13] In its heuristic function, then, narrative operates to deepen, complicate, and even to dismantle our settled beliefs and not simply to calcify them into the surface of mere dogma.

Lionel Trilling laments the seeming erasure of the narrative past from the consciousness of modern persons. As a repository of our values, ideas, and accomplishments, this past, if accessible at all, is regarded as no longer useful in an industrial society whose orientation is toward change, not conservation, toward novelty, not consolidation. What Trilling calls "the unformulated cultural assumption" of the past's uselessness (to my mind, a political assumption operating behind much recent criticism of narrative) has had the

11. While Kermode uses the phrase "paradigmatic rigidity" as a characteristic of myth, I would argue that it applies more aptly to ideology. I will be returning in Chapter 5 to the problem of ideology as it applies to autobiography.

12. J. H. Plumb, *The Death of the Past* (Boston: Houghton Mifflin Co., 1971).

13. Kermode, *The Sense of an Ending*, p. 17.

effect of making all things "weightless," in Nietzsche's word. For a time, the great narrative historians of the nineteenth century maintained "in considerable degree" the "weightiness of things by thickening the past . . . and made it still possible for feet to know the solid earth under them. . . ."[14] Trilling considers modern weightlessness to be part of the legacy of the mutations that the moral life has undergone over several hundred years in its shift of allegiance from the social ideal of sincerity to the existential ideal of authenticity—a legacy, in short, of the nineteenth-century death of God. Viewed from the perspective of this legacy, the efforts of those earlier historians and novelists are regarded with skepticism if not contempt, history now taking the more "scientific" path of structural analysis, the novel reflecting an increasing spatialization of plot.

The death of God, suggested first by Hegel to account for the sentiment underlying religion in the modern age, was for Nietzsche as well as for Hegel a way of describing the loss of anchorage that tradition, the *sensus communis*, once provided. Cut off from the invisible past by the rise of empiricism and its reduction of the real into what is directly observable, man has become, in Kermode's phrase, "man-in-the-midddest," a "thrown" creature who lacks either a firm sense of the past or confidence in the future. But even in this extremity, the need for a sense of the past and of the future is so engrained that in their absence man will invent them: "Men, like poets," he writes, "rush 'into the middest,' *in medias res,* when they are born; they also die in *in medias rebus,* and to make sense of their span they need fictive concords with origins and ends, such as give meaning to lives and poems."[15] A sense of beginnings and of endings is crucial, then, for lives as well as for poems, whether this

14. Trilling, *Sincerity and Authenticity,* p. 138.
15. Kermode, *The Sense of an Ending,* p. 7.

sense be grounded, as for Trilling, in the experience of the narrative past and the *telos* of an imagined future, or whether, as for Kermode, it be simply an existential projection of a need for concords.

The issues at the heart of narrative theory, I would maintain, are religious issues having to do with the sense we can make out of our experience in the world. They cannot be addressed as literary critical issues in any narrow sense, simply as matters of form or structure. Nor can these issues be fully addressed as matters having strictly to do with historiography and the fine-tuning of research methods so as to get at the "truth" of what really happened in the past. Were it the case that these issues could be so contained, either as questions of form or as questions of method, it would be possible to dismiss altogether the problem of tradition as well as to avoid the danger of distorting reality in the interest of achieving comprehensive wholes. We would then have the advantage of immediate access to experience, unencumbered by any prescriptions whatsoever. Autobiography, combining as it does both the fictional and the historical modes of narrative, would be an act of transcription: a matter simply of discovering the truth of the past and of fitting it into a formal design.

Such, however, is not the case, either with respect to autobiography or to narrative in general. Nor would such an essentially atemporal approach to narrative experience be an advantage, since the price of its immediacy is what Hannah Arendt has called the "realm of the invisible." That realm, in my terms, is the depth level of lived experience which, though inaccessible to empirical observation, nonetheless upholds and gives meaning to the "visible, tangible, [and] palpable."[16]

16. Hannah Arendt, *The Life of the Mind: Thinking* (New York: Harcourt Brace Jovanovich, 1978), p. 12.

The fittingness between narrative and life lies, to be sure, in that eidetic compulsion for wholes. But recognizing the temptation to mistake such comprehensiveness for a blueprint of the way things are or should be, I would want to argue that this fittingness lies more productively in the reciprocity of surface and depth that narrative experience enacts. Such a model of narrative behavior is more suggestive of its temporal dimension and the fact that the comprehensiveness it both seeks and virtually exhibits is neither closed nor static. This model also suggests the extent of narrative's affiliation with culture. The move from life to text can be creative and not destructive of the self precisely because it is a cultural or "worldly" transaction and not simply a self-referential one. I will be returning to autobiography's worldliness in my last chapter.

In order to describe the reciprocity of surface and depth that narrative behavior enacts, one needs ask how it is that narrative presents itself or, better, how it is that readers experience narrative as an essentially temporal form. If experience itself has an essentially narrative quality, what is it about narrative experience, as in, say, the novel, that characterizes our "real" experience? Most immediately, the novel captures the one-thing-after-another modality in which we seem to live our day-after-day lives. Indeed, it is this apparent representation of the sheer chronicity of our lives that might be said to authorize the novel's first claim to realism. The successiveness of time is not only the very stuff of the novel, what, in effect, it is made out of, but this successiveness is also the modality in which we seem to experience the novel, page after page, in the act of reading it. There is a "natural" fittingness, then, between the page-after-page of the novel and the day-after-day of our own lives. This *manifest* quality shared by both is what enfranchises the novel's very existence *as* novel.

But, of course, the day-after-day character of the novel has to be undergirded by something more in order for it to make sense. This something more, or what I would call the *latent* dimension of narrative, is necessary for both novel and life to make temporal sense. Mere succession is not sufficient for identity, either personal identity or novel identity. It is at this point that many literary critics, first the formalists and more recently the structuralists, have turned to spatial models to account for this something more, eschewing the diachronicity of both narrative and life in order to highlight their synchronicity. Although the synchronic or spatial-formalistic model serves to gain access to certain features of both narrative and life, it has, I think, tended to distort the dimension of latency or depth in narrative. It is certainly true that depth, as dimensionality, has a spatial character. If time, however, were only a series of instant nows, the thickness of experience would reduce itself to surface. If time were to be experienced only as succession, depth would, in fact, disappear. Not only would it become mere surface (but with nothing to cover); when stretched thin enough, depth would become transparent or nothing at all!

To remove depth altogether from the temporality of experience would, however, make of it something static; even turned "sideways," to continue the visual metaphor, it would be inexperiencable. For at any one time, if one were to stop the clock, it is impossible to see more than a single surface at a time: height and breadth would be accessible to one's retina, but the third dimension would not, except as an optical illusion, much in the way depth is made available through perspective in a painting.

Depth becomes such a *trompe l'oeil* in criticism that conducts its business as a kind of linguistic archeology, excavating and measuring the layers of a presumably self-reflexive system. But since we do *in fact* experience depth as a real thing and not as an illusion, it is necessary to return to temporality in order to account for its way of being, not as a static quantity but as a dynamic quality, not as manifest but as a latent "presence" in our experience.

Ortega's meditation on the forest, which I mentioned in Chapter 1, serves to illustrate not only the latency of depth but also the function of surface in displaying depth to us. To be sure, the forest cannot be seen because of the trees, as the old adage goes. Were it to be fully visible, it would no longer be the forest but a bank of trees. To that degree, the forest exists by virtue of its concealment behind the trees. But it is only by virtue of the trees, what is manifest and thereby surface, that one has a sense of the behind-the-trees. While it is true to say that depth cannot be taken "in hand" as would be the case if it were *mani*fest, it is also true to say that depth *displays* itself *as* surface. To put the matter another way: "To see is to enter a universe of beings which display themselves, and they would not do this if they could not be hidden behind each other or behind me."[17]

Yet another illustration of the reciprocity between surface and depth is Proust's model of the palimpsest, a text that has been built up by overlays of writing. It is this thickness of text, this simultaneity of temporal layers of experience, that Proust was trying to achieve in *Remembrance of Things Past*—a thickness made possible by the immediacy of the present moment, but only as it is pressed on and by the past. The present or surface level of experience is the text as manifest words on the parchment, pulled taut over and given full body by the pressure from beneath or behind it. It is this experience of pressure, unseen but nonetheless present and felt, that gives life to narrative and that, indeed,

17. Merleau-Ponty, *Phenomenology of Perception*, trans. Colin Smith (London: Routledge & Kegan Paul, 1962), p. 68.

gives life to life as well. Depth, then, is unseen but felt and made accessible by the surface made taut.

Surface tautness is an especially prominent feature of modern narrative which seems often to be in revolt against a "linear shape" that "proceeds from point to point from a definite beginning toward a definite end."[18] Attributing this revolt to the "spiritual disequilibrium" of our time, Joseph Frank argues that the novels of Flaubert, Joyce, and Proust represent the "predominance of spatial form." These writers, according to Frank, have adopted a poetic principle from symbolists like Mallarmé and imagists like Ezra Pound who wanted "to create a language of 'absence' rather than of presence—a language in which words negated their objects instead of designating them."[19] What provides the "link" between their earlier poetic experiments and the spatialization of form in the modern novel is, for Frank, "the principle of reflexive reference," a "space-logic" that achieves certain pictorial effects through the use, for example, of juxtaposition. This essentially cinematic technique serves to break up the temporal sequence that is otherwise natural to narrative, slowing it often to a standstill that "tries to approximate the eternal, ethereal tranquility of otherworldly experience."[20]

Rather than ascribing the tautness of narrative surface to such docetic efforts at transcending what Frank calls the "mass and corporeality" of the temporal, I would contend that narratives like *Ulysses* or *Remembrance of Things Past* or even *The Sun Also Rises* (whose surface, though taut, lacks

---

18. Sharon Spencer, *Space, Time and Structure in the Modern Novel* (New York: New York University Press, 1971), p. xxi.

19. Joseph Frank, "Spatial Form in Modern Literature," in *The Widening Gyre: Crisis and Mastery in Modern Literature* (Bloomington: Indiana University Press, 1968), p. 13.

20. Ibid., p. 54.

the slowdown of pictorial detail that fills up the others) are, in fact, dealing with their own "narrativeness." They are narratives, in other words, that can no longer *count on* the dimension of depth as already there. Instead, they raise the question of the possibility of depth. The strategy of these novels should be understood as an effort not to transcend the temporal, but to delve more deeply into it in order to retrieve the dimension of depth.

Autobiography is a mode of fictional and historical narrative that delves into time in order to take up the problem of depth. Ever since Augustine's *Confessions,* time has been recognized as the subject matter of autobiography—although not always as its medium, as I am arguing it is. The ordinariness of time is suggested in Thoreau's homely claim that "time is the stream I go afishing in." Not so ordinary, however, is his surprising suggestion that the bait he would use is the self. He is not fishing in time, then, for the purpose of catching the self and rescuing it from time's flux, which so many critics would define as a central goal of autobiography. The self is rather the bait Thoreau would use to catch something else in the medium of time. And what he would catch is Walden Pond, the "earth's eye" that represents for Thoreau reality itself. This eye is a mode of perception *into* which he would look for the purpose of measuring the "depth of his own nature," not an eye out of which he could achieve a worldless perspective.

With himself as bait, then, Thoreau will go afishing in time. He "hooks" himself for this expedition into autobiography in the opening page of his account when he adopts the first-person standpoint of speaking: "We commonly do not remember that it is, after all, always the first person that is speaking." With this reminder that would otherwise seem to be redundant in the context of *auto-*biography, Thoreau is calling attention, first of all, to the fact that speaking is the beginning of autobiography. Not only is language the *matter* of autobiography, but the self as language (the flesh made word, if you will) is its *form* as well.

To view autobiography as simply a report on past events is to overlook the fact that autobiography takes place in the present. Thoreau's present-participal formulation, the first person *speaking,* represents the *nunc stans* of taking up one's situation in time. One does not thereby fix or close down one's life in the present moment as though speaking arises *de nouveau,* thus serving to arrest time in some static category. To understand autobiography as an act of speaking is to underscore its full temporality. Speaking takes place in time, constituting itself in the present, but deriving from the past and projecting itself into the future. As a single movement which incorporates that past into the present and "welds" that present to a future, speaking reenacts "the temporal style of the world."[21]

It is by means of language that life is always in the process of catching up with itself. Catching up, however, is a matter not only of catching *back* to the past whose horizon makes room for the present, but of catching *forward* as well, to the horizon of the future where " 'reality' always stands" as "observed and feared or, at any rate, [as] still undecided possibilities."[22]

The autobiographical act of bringing life to language involves a temporal gathering of what Hannah Arendt calls "the absent tenses," the "no-more" of the past and the "not-yet" of the future, into the fullness of the present.[23] The autobiographical present, however, is not to be understood as a spatial habitat which is above or immune to the flux of time. *To speak one's life is, rather, to take up occupancy within the mobile setting of time as depth.*

21. See Merleau-Ponty, *Phenomenology of Perception,* pp. 421–24.
22. Ibid., p. 101.
23. Arendt, *The Life of the Mind: Thinking,* p. 211.

Were one to look at autobiography as a spatial act, language, it could be said, takes up that space and fills it, but not like filling a vessel that would otherwise be empty. The ever-present background of speech means that space is never simply empty or neutral. It is occupied and directed and therefore more accurately to be understood as *place*. In this respect, *Walden* is as much an autobiographical expedition into space as into time. Spatial imagery, in fact, abounds in Thoreau's work along with those boundaries that are presumed, often mistakenly, to define or more often to confine that space. When Thoreau records his desire to speak "somewhere without bounds," he is working not toward some boundless eternity of transcendental standpoint. One cannot, after all, wedge one's feet into everywhere. He is looking, rather, for that *one place* from which he will have access to everywhere. Or, as he puts it, he is searching for that "one fact" which if "you stand right fronting . . . face to face . . . you will see the sun glimmer on both its surfaces . . . and feel its sweet edge dividing you through the heart and marrow, and so you will happily conclude your mortal career."[24] That one fact he discovers in the coming of spring and, in particular, in the thawing of the sand bank at the side of the railroad track. It is here, in this "one actual phenomenon," that he experiences the true nature of depth in all its fullness—a fullness which comes to expression as the *dehiscence of time* and which transforms space into sacred place.[25]

In the *Journal* entry of September 5, 1851, shortly before he undertook his major revision of *Walden*, Thoreau records his dream of achieving "a return to the primitive analogical

24. Henry Thoreau, *Walden*, ed. J. Lyndon Shanley (Princeton: Princeton University Press, 1971), p. 98. Subsequent citations will be indicated by page numbers directly following the quotations in my text.

25. See Merleau-Ponty's discussion of time as dehiscence in *Phenomenology of Perception*, pp. 419 ff.

and derivative sources of words."[26] Such an achievement was a goal held in common by the Transcendentalist circle which regularly gathered in Elizabeth Palmer Peabody's Boston bookstore during the 1830s and 40s. The influence of German Idealism and Swedenborgian correspondences was evident in their attempts to formulate a philosophy of "natural language" which would contravene the Lockean understanding of words as arbitrary signs invented for social communication. Most persuasive for the Transcendentalists' understanding of language was Johann Gottfried von Herder's thesis, in *The Spirit of Hebrew Poetry* (which Miss Peabody had reviewed), that the roots of language are to be found in nature itself. This thesis seems to find expression in Thoreau's famous passage on style in his essay "Walking":

> Where is the literature which gives expression to Nature? He would be a poet who could impress the winds and streams into his service, to speak for him; who nailed words to their primitive senses, as farmers drive down stakes in the spring, which the frost has heaved; who derived his words as often he used them—transplanting them to his page with earth adhering to their roots. . . .[27]

These lines on the poet's activity recall much of Thoreau's conduct in the first sixteen chapters of *Walden:* As expressed in the "Walking" passage, the forceful nailing and driving fulfills the requirement Thoreau makes of himself as well as of his readers when he admonishes them to live life *deliberately.* Not only must he and his readers bring con-

26. Bradford Torrey and Francis H. Allen, eds., *The Journal of Henry D. Thoreau* I [fourteen volumes, bound as two] (New York: Dover Publications, 1962), p. 462.

27. Henry Seidel Canby, ed., *The Works of Thoreau* (Boston: Houghton Mifflin Company, 1946), p. 676.

scious purpose to their unthinking lives; such purpose must be carried out with the near-military vigor he brings to that familiar statement of purpose in *Walden:* "I went to the woods because I wished to live deliberately, to front only the essential facts of life; . . . to live so sturdily and Spartan-like as to put to rout all that was not life" (90–91). The Spartan warrior in this early *Walden* passage is the same commander who, in the "Walking" essay, would "impress the winds and streams into his service."

But there is yet another part of this passage on natural style, this one having to do with the effect of the words on the "faithful reader" rather than with the treatment they would have at the hands of the poet. In the second half of the passage, Thoreau writes that these

> words were so true and fresh and natural that they would appear to expand like the buds at the approach of spring, though they lay half smothered between two musty leaves in a library—aye, to bloom and bear fruit there, after their kind, annually, for the faithful reader, in sympathy with surrounding Nature.[28]

In contrast to the downward thrust of nailing and driving that is intended to anchor the poet's words in the substratum of Nature—a thrust that suggests a calculated decisiveness and not a little violence—the words appear to the "faithful reader" in quite another way: as emerging and expanding in a process that, far from being abrupt and the result of deliberate planning, is slow and spontaneous.

Here, then, we have a completion of the twofold activity that characterizes the *Walden* experiment. As I shall demonstrate in the remainder of this chapter, Thoreau's autobiographical experiment in *Walden* has to do with his becoming this "faithful reader." He meets that goal in his

28. Ibid., pp. 676–77.

"reading" of spring, an experience which constitutes for him an event of language that discloses the temporal style of the world. This style is the mediator of depth; the coming of spring constitutes that "one fact" which reveals "the infinite extent of our relations."

There are many passages in *Walden* where Thoreau makes quite clear his interest in language: "It would seem," he writes in a later chapter, "as if the very language of our parlors would lose all its nerve and degenerate into *parlaver* wholly, our lives pass at such remoteness from its symbols . . ." (244–45). Much earlier, he has already put the question, "Who knows but if men constructed their dwellings with their own hands, and provided food for themselves and families simply and honestly enough, the poetic faculty would be universally developed, as birds universally sing when they are so engaged" (46). Midway between these two passages, in "The Beanfield," he remarks, ". . . some must work in fields if only for the sake of tropes and expression, to serve a parable-maker one day" (162). What is striking in all three instances is the way Thoreau grounds his interest in language, whether it be the "language of our parlors" or the "poetic faculty," in the ordinariness of daily experience, particularly house-building. Further highlighted in the correspondence between language and house-building (and cultivating beans) is the notion of foundation, which seems the very source of this inner-outer process. And it is here that the reciprocal relation between language and depth becomes more clear. Not only does language come out of depth, but language ("I want to make the earth speak beans") is what puts one back in touch with depth as well. On his beans, Thoreau writes, "They attached me to the earth, and so I got strength like Antaeus" (155).

Language, then, derives its power, Antaeus-like, from its rootedness in the earth. And conversely, one gains access to this rootedness by way of language, out of those forms of expression (house-building, bean-growing, poetry-making) that make manifest, bring to the surface, the under-the-soil source of all true expression.

There are countless examples of the foundation metaphor throughout *Walden*. It would seem, in fact, that the central project of the book could be described as the efforts —almost always deliberate, as I have already noted—to reach those foundations, to "live deep," as Thoreau puts it. These efforts can be seen in the early lyrical passage on wedging one's feet downward:

> Let us settle ourselves, and work and wedge our feet downward through the mud and slush of opinion, and prejudice, and tradition, and delusion, and appearance, that alluvian which covers the globe, through Paris and London, through New York and Boston and Concord, through church and state, through poetry and philosophy and religion till we come to a hard bottom and rocks in place, which we can call reality, and say, This is, and no mistake. . . . Be it life or death, we crave only reality (97–98).

In more detailed and literal description, Thoreau's "ontological scavenger hunt" can be noted in the soundings of the bottom of Walden Pond.[29] "It is remarkable," he had observed, "how long men will believe in the bottomlessness of a pond without taking the trouble to sound it" (285). Having himself taken such trouble in the dead of winter and by means of a hole cut in the ice, Thoreau seems to have edged closer to that "one fact," to the "This is, and no mistake" that he had earlier announced as the goal of his wedging. His final testimony in "Conclusion," that "there is a solid bottom everywhere," would seem to complete his

29. Walter Benn Michaels, *"Walden's* False Bottoms," *Glyph* I, eds. Samuel Weber and Henry Sussman (Baltimore: The Johns Hopkins University Press, 1977), p. 136.

experiment and make it possible for Thoreau to leave Walden for other lives.

But the sounding he was able to take—the Pond, he recorded, was "exactly one hundred and two feet deep"— is *not* the "one fact" that could bring to an end his "mortal career." As Thoreau himself is quick to note of this "remarkable depth for so small an area," it is still the case that "[w]hile men believe in the infinite some ponds will be thought to be bottomless" (287). Notwithstanding the Cartesian-like probing of his wedging passage, the *"point d'appui"* that he would achieve depends not so much on *what* he sees as the *way* he sees it. He is interested, he says, in "carv[ing] and paint[ing] the very atmosphere and medium through which we look. . . ." Or as he puts it in his *Journal* entry of September 13, 1852, "What I need is not to look at all, but a true sauntering of the eye."[30]

Taken alone, this entry is misleading and actually contradicts the "habit of attention" to which Thoreau refers in an earlier part of this entry, a habit he has "to such excess that my senses get no rest, but suffer from a constant strain." The strain of attention is evident throughout his *Walden* account. The moralist who complains that "[o]ur life is frittered away by detail" is at the same time the naturalist who painstakingly records in minutest detail the behavior of hooting owls, the size and density of animal skins, and the freezing dates of Walden Pond.

As for the itinerancy implied by the "true sauntering of the eye," Thoreau recorded elsewhere his belief that "to appreciate a single phenomenon, you must camp down beside it as for life. . . ."[31] Such a camping down we find, for instance, at Thoreau's woodpile site from which he observes, much like Swift's Gulliver in the miniaturized world

30. Torrey and Allen, *The Journal of Henry D. Thoreau* I, p. 350.
31. Quoted by Quentin Anderson, "Practical and Visionary Americans," *The American Scholar* XLV (1976): 409.

of the Lilliputians, the "internicine war" between the armies of ants, "the red republicans on the one hand, the black imperialists on the other."

Applied biographically to what he does at Walden, then, the statement that contrasts looking with the sauntering eye makes little sense. But as a statement regarding his interest in language as the "very atmosphere and medium through which we look," it is central to his autobiographical goal. That goal is "to lay the foundation of a true expression." The coming of spring and, in particular, Thoreau's observations on the thawing of the sand bank at the edge of the railroad track disclose such a foundation.

In that same 1852 *Journal* entry he writes, "Go not to the object, let it come to you." To be sure, Thoreau must sustain that state of "morning wakefulness" and "infinite expectation" which qualify him for the "highest art," namely, "to affect the quality of the day." At the same time, he must break the "habit of attention" that tends to domesticate "the vastness and strangeness of Nature." Nothing short of total disorientation will accomplish this break and make possible the "wise passivity" that contrasts so strikingly with the military deliberations which superintend his activities leading up to spring. "Not till we are lost," he writes—and the New Testament allusion is unmistakable— "in other words, not till we have lost the world, do we begin to find ourselves, and realize where we are and the infinite extent of our relations" (171). Having tried to make a home *in* Nature by going in so many ways to the object, Thoreau's autobiography will finally be a home *for* Nature when he lets the object come to him.

Dramatizing Nature "in full blast" and representing the fullest portrayal of the relation between language and depth, the passages on the thawing of the sand bank bring together all the major themes and movements of the book: the temporal unfolding of the hours, days, and seasons, and the spatial unlayering of geography, history, geology, and myth. At the conclusion of his observations he is able finally to announce, "[t]here is nothing inorganic." And having experienced "this one hillside" that "illustrated the principle of all the operations of Nature," Thoreau can report:

> The earth is not a mere fragment of dead history, stratum upon stratum like the leaves of a book, to be studied by geologists and antiquaries chiefly, but living poetry like the leaves of the trees, which precede flowers and fruit,—not a fossil earth, but a living earth . . . (309).

Spring's arrival announces itself first from a distance, in the "startling whoop" of ice breaking on the Pond, a sound as "loud as artillery" that Thoreau hears in the night. He had been attuned for this sound from the beginning of his sojourn: "One attraction in coming to the woods to live was that I should have the leisure and opportunity to see the Spring come in" (302). All of his arrangements, one can now see in retrospect, have been geared to this event: the building of a house to conserve that "vital heat" which will find its correspondence in Nature's "great furnace," the cultivation of morning wakefulness when "there is a dawn in me" that will enable so close an observation of Nature as to "anticipate" her, the meditation on getting lost in the woods so as to "begin to find ourselves, and realize where we are and the infinite extent of our relations." Preparatory as well have been Thoreau's deliberate efforts to find the solid bottom: his "wedging" his feet "downward" and his cutting through the frozen ice to sound the Pond, along with his careful excavating and recording of the layers of historical and mythical events (from the building of the railroad back to the prelapsarian creation of Walden Pond) that have preceded his own coming to the Pond and have served to hold him in place. All of this, "the perpetual instilling and drenching of the reality that surrounds us," has served to ready him for spring. And what he finally comes to experience more than confirms his credo, announced much earlier in "What I lived for," that "[t]he universe constantly and obediently answers to our conceptions; whether we travel fast or slow, the track is laid for us . . ." (98).

But what is finally most significant about his experience of spring is the extent to which its "extra-vagance" outstrips his conceptions, leading him at the end of his account to conclude that "[t]he universe is wider than our views of it" (320). For unlike his earlier deliberations, by which he sought intentionally to peel away the layers that conceal the depth of Nature, the thawing of the sand bank reveals Nature's *own* intentions. The dramatic movement of spring is upward and outward—"The very globe continually transcends and translates itself, and becomes winged in its orbit"—a counter to the winter inwardness and the downwardness of Thoreau's wedging and sounding.

What the *manifest*ation of Nature in spring has to suggest, *contra* classical autobiography theory, is that the surfacing of depth by way of language is *not* the losing of depth but, on the contrary, that it is the bringing of depth to fullest expression. But what is more, spring testifies to what is at the heart of depth's concealment, namely, that *depth exists in anticipation of becoming surface,* lying in wait to burst forth in the manifest language of leaves: "No wonder that the earth expresses itself outwardly in leaves, it *so labors* with the idea inwardly" (306, *italics mine*).

What Thoreau comes to realize constitutes the very center of the autobiographical project, operating both as its source and its *telos.* He has finally come to experience in the dehiscence of depth what has been all along the "already there," that anchorage in temporality which enables him to engage in such a project in the first place. What initially pre-tended itself as necessarily concealed below the surface, a surface through which his early strategies—both physical and linguistic—were designed to penetrate, finally presents itself *as* surface, there all the while but awaiting that *gaze* which could see it, a seeing made possible by the "atmosphere and medium" of the language of Nature that Thoreau has made his own.

Thoreau had earlier observed of the surface of Walden Pond that "not a pickerel or shiner picks an insect from this smooth surface but it manifestly disturbs the equilibrium of the whole lake. . . . Not a fish can leap or an insect fall on the pond but it is thus reported in circling dimples, the lines of beauty, as it were the constant welling up of its fountain, the gentle pulsing of its life, the heaving of its breast" (187, 188). The tautness of *Walden*'s narrative surface, compressing as it does the actual experience of several years into one and harkening back to Thoreau's earliest memories at the age of four, itself records such minute undulations.[32] And like the lake which is the "landscape's most beautiful and expressive feature," Thoreau's autobiographical narrative is the "earth's eye, looking into which the beholder measures the depth [of all things, including] . . . his own nature" (186).

If Nature is the foundation of "true expression," there is finally no going behind language to its origins. Nature, or reality, makes itself known only through its own language, its speaking "beans" or its expression in leaves. The founda-

---

32. Thoreau writes of his childhood memory of the Pond: "It is one of the oldest scenes stamped on my memory" (155). I might add that the writing-history of *Walden,* which is compressed in the account, contributes to the density of its textual pressure. As J. Lyndon Shanley and others have pointed out, *Walden* represents the condensation of seven or eight years of revisions. Its materials go back to *Journal* entries that date from April 1839, a good six years before Thoreau took up residence at the Pond. See Shanley, *The Making of Walden* (Chicago: University of Chicago Press, 1957) and Mutlu Konuk Blasing, *The Art of Life: Studies in American Autobiographical Literature* (Austin: University of Texas Press, 1977).

tion that Thoreau himself can lay is constituted by the interpretive act of his own autobiography—an act of faithful reading more than an act of deliberate writing. In words that are "derived" as often as they are "used," he can become that "faithful reader, in [such] sympathy with surrounding Nature" that his own life can be synechdochical for the lives of others, not in providing the exact pattern to which those others must fit their own, but in urging other acts of reading. Only in the risk of interpretation—"what we have to stand on tip-toe to read and devote our most alert and wakeful hours to" (104)—will men and women be rescued from their "quiet desperation" and assured "[t]here is more day to dawn."

3

The Autobiographical Perspective

THE HERMENEUTIC OF LANDSCAPE
IN WORDSWORTH'S "TINTERN ABBEY"

The burdens of the world
on my back
lighten the world
not a whit while
removing them greatly decreases my specific
gravity.
    —A. R. Ammons, "Correction"

    Georges Gusdorf writes of the combined fear and fascination that attend the autobiographical shift of attention from so-called outside to inside space:

> If space outside—the stage of the world—is a light, clear space where everyone's behavior, movements, and motives are quite plain on first sight, space inside is shadowy in its very essence. The subject who seizes on himself for object inverts the natural direction of attention; it appears that in acting thus he violates certain secret taboos of human nature. Sociology, depth psychology, [and] psychoanalysis have revealed the complex and agonizing sense that the encounter of a man with his image carries. The image is another "myself," a double of my being, but more fragile and vulnerable, invested with a sacred character which makes it at once fascinating and frightening. Narcissus, con-

templating his face in the fountain's depth, is so fascinated with the apparition that he would die bending toward himself.[1]

The fear of violating these "secret taboos of human nature" may well account for the kinds of nervous beginnings one finds in so many modern autobiographies. Up to about 1800, the uneasiness of inverting the attention from outside to inside space could be "covered" by what had long been established in the tradition of spiritual autobiography. The religious autobiographer, an Augustine, a Jonathan Edwards, a George Fox, could regard the exploration of the inner self as an injunction from God Himself. The opening pages of his confession or journal could naturally assume a conventional formula of *apologia* that combined explanation with excuse. "Yet suffer me to speak, since I speak to Thy mercy, and not to scornful man."[2] In directing his confessions to God and not to "scornful man," Augustine can relate the details of a life that, presumably, God already knows better than the confessor. Some of Rousseau's romanticized confession fourteen hundred years later contains a virtual parody of Augustine's beginning: "I have bared my secret soul as Thou thyself hast seen it, Eternal Being! So let the numberless legion of my fellow man gather round me, and hear my confessions."[3]

In what one critic has called the first American autobiography,[4] Benjamin Franklin can make use of the conven-

1. Georges Gusdorf, "Conditions and Limits of Autobiography," in *Autobiography: Essays Theoretical and Critical*, ed. James Olney (Princeton: Princeton University Press, 1980), p. 32.

2. Augustine, Bishop of Hippo, *The Confessions of Saint Augustine*, trans. E. B. Pusey (New York: E. P. Dutton & Co., 1907), p. 1.

3. Jean-Jacques Rousseau, *The Confessions*, trans. J. M. Cohen (Baltimore: Penguin Books, 1954), p. 17.

4. James M. Cox, "Autobiography and America," in *Aspects of Narrative*, ed. J. Hillis Miller (New York: Columbia University Press, 1971), pp. 143–72.

tion of the conduct book, addressing his autobiography to his son—even though that son is already in his forties and a statesman himself—in order to convert an otherwise vain account of Franklin's successes into an edifying set of instructions for the young. By the time Thoreau writes his mid-nineteenth-century autobiographical account in *Walden,* he must half-jokingly apologize that "I should not talk so much about myself if there were anybody else whom I knew as well."

It is against the long tradition of spiritual autobiography that, from the late eighteenth century to the present, more recent autobiographies have placed themselves. These works no longer utilize so comfortably the trope of religious pilgrimage; they more naturally, if more nervously, use the trope of the stage, which had replaced the earlier pilgrimage trope sometime during the Renaissance.[5] The metaphor of the stage allows for the variety of roles that a less fixed social structure and a more heteronomous set of religious views both permit and, in fact, enjoin.

The greater flexibility of possible openings, along with the anxiety produced by the very increase of options, highlights the problem of *placing* the self which is so central to modern autobiography. To be sure, the question of location constitutes a near-obsession even as early as Augustine's *Confessions* in the late fourth century. By the time of the famous opening of Proust's autobiographical novel, however, neither the reader nor the narrator is quite sure of where the young—or is it the older?—Marcel is located. The ambiguity of placement in *Remembrance of Things Past* is, of course, intentional, since it introduces a key strategy for the entire novel which asks the large questions about where real life can be presumed to exist in both space and time.

5. See Paul Delaney, *British Autobiography in the Seventeenth Century* (London: Routledge & Kegan Paul, 1969).

The problem of placement initiates the second level of autobiography wherein the adumbration of a perspective is at issue. The space that autobiography occupies is, however, the *cultural space* which already combines what Gusdorf calls "inside" and "outside." Such being the case, the issue of autobiographical perspective rests not so much on a question of boundaries to be transcended—the boundary, for instance, between the reputedly private space of confession and the public space of memoir; the question has rather to do with the autobiographer's laying claim to the cultural territory he or she already occupies and in such a way that "space" is transformed into "place" or, in the formulation of Ortega y Gasset, that *"milieu"* can become "landscape":

> I fought against the idea that man inhabits a *milieu*. Because a *milieu* is no specific place, it is everywhere. And what seemed essential to me was man's non-ubiquity, his "servitude to a plot of ground." The *milieu*, once I was able to see it as my circumstances, became a landscape. Landscape, unlike the more abstract *milieu*, is a function of a specific man. The same corner of earth becomes as many landscapes as there are men or nations to transverse it. . . . It is not simply that the land makes man, but that man *elects* his land, that is, his landscape, that portion of the planet where he finds his ideal or life-project symbolically prefigured. People often forget that man is a nomadic animal, that he is always potentially migratory. This ability to leave, so basic in man that it finds its supreme expression in suicide, forces us to explain all settling-down by an appeal to free and personal reasons.[6]

6. José Ortega y Gasset, *Phenomenology and Art*, trans. Philip W. Silver (New York: W. W. Norton & Co., 1975), p. 71.

Autobiography, then, is the act of "settling-down" or, in Thoreau's famous image, of wedging one's feet downward. It represents an act both of discovery and creation that involves, at the same time, the movement of the self *in* the world, recognizing that "the land makes man," and the movement of the self *into* the world, recognizing as well that "man elects his land."

"In recounting my story," as Gusdorf says, "I take the longest path, but this path which goes round my life leads me the more surely from me to myself."[7] In electing the cultural territory that I have mentioned, the autobiographer is taking the "path which goes round [his or her] life," thereby situating that life in the *sensus communis* out of which its story can be told and to which the self is restored in the telling. What the self comes to understand in the act of autobiography is not simply a projection of that self; nor, on the other hand, is it the usurping of the self and its freedom by the "authority" of the world. The relation between self and world is always to be seen as a creative dialectic between participation and distantiation.[8]

But it is just here that there arises a set of problems in the negotiations between self and world, since the dialectic between participation and distantiation, or discovery and creation, is always in danger of being collapsed toward one side or another: on the one side is the tendency toward idealism and the problem of the imperial self; on the other side is the tendency toward empiricism and the problem of the self's "habituation" by the world.

Both of these problems are, to be sure, modern—the result of what Karl Weintraub calls the "specifically modern

7. Gusdorf, "Conditions and Limits of Autobiography," p. 38.
8. Once again, I am indebted to the work of Paul Ricoeur for the terms *participation* and *distantiation,* which are central to his theory of interpretation.

form of self-conception" as "individuality."[9] At whatever point one would want to date the beginning of the modern period, these problems come into sharpest focus in the romantic era, concomitant with the full flowering of the autobiographic genre as we know it today. And it is in the poetic program of William Wordsworth, as I will try to show in the remainder of this chapter, that the self-world problem, in both of its forms and in direct relation to the issue of autobiographical perspective, receives head-on confrontation.

In his 1802 poem, "Resolution and Independence," William Wordsworth is contending with what he calls elsewhere the "abyss of idealism" that lies at the heart of romanticism, namely, the tendency of the self to fit the world into its own view of reality.[10] Wordsworth has chosen a good test case in the poem's Leech-gatherer, whose initial appearance lacks the clear outline which could resist absorption into the typically Wordsworthian scene. Not only does his static figure, "not all alive nor dead," offer no clear delineation that would set him off from the rest of the idealized setting—the lonely moor with its mist and rocks in place, which seems to engulf him; from afar the old man appears to be a rock himself, a "thing endued with sense" (l.61). Even closer up, the feeble man, "propped, limbs, body, and pale face,/Upon a long grey staff of shaven wood" (ll. 71-72), is immobile, patiently staring into the stagnant pool, as presumably he has done year after year, looking for the catch of leeches that provide his livelihood.

9. Karl Joachim Weintraub, *The Value of the Individual: Self and Circumstance in Autobiography* (Chicago: University of Chicago Press, 1978), p. xiv.

10. Quotations from "Resolution and Independence" will come from Wordsworth's final edition of the poem (1859–60) which appears in *The Poetical Works of William Wordsworth*, ed. E. De Selincourt (Oxford: Clarendon Press, 1944), Vol. 2, pp. 235–40.

The leeches, too, lead a passive life as we can imagine them attached to their environment, rock or human body, steadily sucking into their bodies whatever substance feeds them, lichens or blood, their activity but an instinctual reflex of holding on. Unlike the Wordsworthian poet-figure in "Tintern Abbey," they and their gatherer neither "half create" nor even "perceive." The symbiotic relation of passive existence between the old man and his "crop" seems unalterably fixed in the scene by the middle of the poem: "Motionless as a cloud the old Man stood,/That hearest not the loud winds when they call;/And moveth all together, if it move at all" (ll. 75–77).

The career of the romantic poet is exactly the opposite even though his trade might parallel, at first, the Leech-gatherer's in their mutual absorption of the world around them. But this initial absorption directs itself to a very different end for the poet: the taking in of the world is but the preliminary stage for disgorging it in quite another form. The poet is called to transform the static, mechanistic, and deadening universe of Newtonian science into a dynamic and resurrected organism, infusing it with the life that the poet can both detect in and inject into all things, rocks as well as rolling streams.

In recalling the young Chatterton, a promising poet who committed suicide at the age of seventeen, Wordsworth, at the beginning of the poem, seems to fear the possible consequences of such a program whose stakes along with whose calling are very high indeed: "We Poets in our youth begin in gladness;/But thereof come in the end despondency and madness" (ll. 48–49). The poet-priest who would officiate at the transubstantiating sacrament of inert machine into active organism risks much.

In the remarks he made on his great Intimations Ode, Wordsworth paints a clearer picture of the threat that he faces in his poetic negotiation with the world:

> I was often unable to think of external things as having external existence, and I communed with all that I saw as something not apart from, but inherent in, my own immaterial nature. Many times while going to school have I grasped at a wall or tree to recall myself from this abyss of idealism to reality.[11]

He clearly recognizes in this passage the dangers lying in wait for the poet. And it is these dangers he is squarely confronting in his account of the Leech-gatherer whose own existence as an autonomous living agent is at stake, along with the large and revolutionary poetic program that Wordsworth has undertaken. The dilemma is clear and dramatic: Can the poet bring nature to consciousness without resorting to an imperialization of reality, without, in other words, so projecting his own sense of life that he simply engorges the world around him, ending up with a soplipsistic and maddening universe of self?

This dilemma, of course, lies at the heart of the autobiographical act. There is no blinking the fact that the autobiographer runs the risk of Narcissus, both in seeing his own reflection in everything around him—an illusory triumph of the self that can thereby lose contact with the dimension of otherness which alone can hold him in place—and, even more precipitously, in leaning over himself so intently that he falls and drowns in his own reflection.

In view of such epistemological complexity, my choice of Wordsworth's "Tintern Abbey" as a particularly suggestive instance of the self's placement in modern autobiography might seem anomalous. His poem strikes one, after all, as surprisingly simple and straightforward. It is a poem, moreover, that has been praised for its sense of *thereness*, not

11. See David Perkins, ed., *English Romantic Writers* (New York: Harcourt, Brace, & World, 1967), p. 279.

only in its rich, even palpable presentation of place, but in the firmness with which the speaker in the poem wins and holds this place as his own. There is, in other words, a transparency about the poem, both in its clarity of objective description and in its more subjective analysis of the poet's way of seeing and, even more strikingly, his way of hearing.

I do not intend to argue that this effect of transparency is finally deceptive. It is rather my contention that the transparent, or what, in the "Preface" to *The Lyrical Ballads,* Wordsworth calls the familiar, is both the subject matter and the problem of the poem. In its conversational style and the steadiness of its movement, the poem makes us value what Karl Kroeber calls "the subliminal effects of the familiar," the "recognition that the importance of the familiar lies in its manifestation of some rhythmic continuity necessary to our life."[12] In "Tintern Abbey," Wordsworth must win his way to the familiar by resisting a pre-fabricated "schema" that tempts him with a too-easy harmony purchased at the cost of lived experience. In "Resolution and Independence," the familiar awaits him in the ordinary experience of the Leech-gatherer who saves the poet from the maddening illusion of being without any orienting schema at all—the illusion, in other words, that it is only in the interiority of his own consciousness that any leverage on reality can be found. Although the latter poem was composed four years after "Tintern Abbey," it can be said, in our present reading of the poems, that "Resolution and Independence" provides the frame of acceptance or the fiduciary context within which the familiar can be celebrated.

This later poem sets the stage, then, for a fuller understanding of the earlier one, as I am in the middle of arguing.

12. Karl Kroeber, *Romantic Landscape Vision: Constable and Wordsworth* (Madison: University of Wisconsin Press, 1975), p. 33.

I left off that argument at the end of stanza eleven where there was established a symbiotic relation between the gatherer and his leeches in the shared passivity of their brute holding onto life. The movement of the poem has momentarily come to a halt, leaving the reader (and the poet) with a tableaux of nature's endurability. But this stasis is not enough for the Wordsworth who, while recognizing the risks of imperialism in the self's moving out into the world, must, at all costs, bring nature "to speech." Having brought the poem to a stand-still, a stoppage all the more striking in its contrast with the "roaring" winds and running hares of the opening stanzas and with the abrupt plunge of the poet's mood from high delight to low dejection, Wordsworth starts up the poem once again in stanza twelve:

> At length, himself unsettling, he the pond
> Stirred with his staff, and fixedly did look
> Upon the muddy water, which he conned,
> As if he had been reading in a book:
> And now a stranger's privilege I took;
> And, drawing to his side, to him did say,
> "This morning gives us promise of a glorious day"
>   (ll. 78–84).

The Leech-gatherer makes the first move, "unsettling" himself and "stirring" the pond. He "conned" the "muddy water," the poet now observes, "As if he had been reading a book." The contrast between the heretofore passive gaze of the old man and the activity of reading a book introduces the poet's own renewed activity, an interpretive activity that will end with yet another moment of stillness in the final stanza. This second moment, however, will be the stillness of active resolution, not of passive stasis:

I could have laughed to scorn to find
In that decrepit Man so firm a mind.
"God," said I, "be my help and stay secure;
I'll think of the Leech-gatherer on the lonely
    moor!" (ll. 137–40).

In between the twelfth and final stanzas, the poet learns something of the old man's life, a story, Wordsworth writes to Sara Hutchinson (who is shortly to become his sister-in-law), "in which I was rescued from my dejection and despair almost as an interposition of Providence."[13] In this same letter, he chides her insensitivity at regarding the Leech-gatherer's speech as merely "tedious": "It is in the character of the old man to tell his story in a manner which an *impatient* reader must necessarily feel as tedious," he remonstrates. "But Good God! Such a figure, in such a place, a pious self-respecting, miserably infirm, and Old Man telling such a tale!"[14]

The tale is one of perseverance, indeed of the resolution and independence that characterize so many of Wordsworth's figures: the old Cumberland beggar, the shepherd Michael, the old soldier of *The Prelude,* and the rejected Martha Ray of "The Thorn." But, as Geoffrey Hartman suggests, "Resolution and Independence," like all of Wordsworth's "greater lyrics," is a poem, both in mode and in subject, of "self-confrontation."[15] That self-confrontation is

13. See Perkins, *English Romantic Writers,* p. 353.
14. Ibid.
15. Geoffrey H. Hartman, *Wordsworth's Poetry 1787–1814* (New Haven: Yale University Press, 1964), pp. 272–73. See also Harold Bloom, *The Visionary Company: A Reading of English Romantic Poetry,* revised and enlarged edition (Ithaca: Cornell University Press, 1971), pp. 164–70. Bloom suggests that Wordsworth's Leech-gatherer represents "the primeval quality of life itself" or, in Wallace Stevens' words, which Bloom quotes, "the gray particularity of man's self."

made possible, paradoxical as it may seem, by his resisting and overcoming the self's imperialism in what Hartman calls "the steadying recognition" that the poet gains from his chance encounter with the Leech-gatherer, a recognition of the old man's existence as such, or, in the poem's terms which introduce him, "a something given." As Wordsworth puts the matter in his letter to Sara Hutchinson:

> A person reading this Poem with feelings like mine will have been awed and controuled [*sic*], expecting almost something spiritual or supernatural—What is brought forward? "A lonely place, a Pond" "by which an old man *was*, far from all house or home"—not stood, not sat, but *"was"*—the figure presented in the most naked simplicity possible.[16]

The aim of Wordsworth's entire poetic program was the presentation of such simplicity: "the simple produce of the common day" communicated "by words/Which speak of nothing more than what we are," as he wrote in the 1800 "Prospectus" of *The Excursion*. His choice of such figures as the Leech-gatherer, Wordsworth tells us in his "Preface to the Second Edition of *The Lyrical Ballads*," rests on his belief that

> in that condition [of "humble and rustic life"], the essential passions of the heart find a better soil in which they can attain their maturity, are less under restraint, and speak a plainer and more emphatic language; because in that condition of life our elementary feelings co-exist in a state of greater simplicity, and, consequently, may be more accurately contemplated, and more forcibly communicated. . . .[17]

16. Perkins, *English Romantic Writers*, p. 353.
17. De Selincourt, *The Poetical Works of William Wordsworth*, Volume 2, pp. 386–87.

He is referring here as much to the "greater simplicity" that the poet himself can achieve in his accurate contemplation as he is to the simplicity exemplified in his poems' characters. Moreover, his poetry is designed to recall the reader to the same accuracy of contemplation.

William Hazlett's comment on the Lake Poet, not altogether complimentary, recognizes Wordsworth's unique achievement: "No one has shown the same imagination," Hazlett wrote, "in raising trifles into importance."[18] M. H. Abrams, in his magisterial *Natural Supernaturalism,* considers this achievement as nothing less than revolutionary, marking Wordsworth as the "poetical Jacobean of his generation." His "essential originality" lies for Abrams "in his ability to perceive the inherent sublimity in the common and the lowly, and the charismatic power in the trivial and the mean."[19]

What is new in Wordsworth's poetry is not only his presenting what, for the eighteenth century, were new subjects for poetry, thereby extending its range to the ordinary. As Wordsworth himself realized, this was simply to return poetry to a much earlier scriptural tradition. What was new was his providing a new way of *seeing* these subjects, a move, Abrams calls it, from "physical optics" to "spiritual optics." By such a move, the reader, too, would be able to see them as they are.

For Wordsworth, the difficulty lay just here: to "communicate to the reader an active '*power*,' " as he put it in his *Essay, Supplementary to the Preface* (1815), "to cooperate with the 'powers' of the poet as applied 'to objects on which they

18. Quoted from "Mr. Wordsworth," in *The Spirit of the Age* (1825) by M. H. Abrams, *Natural Supernaturalism: Tradition and Revolution in Romantic Literature* (New York: W. W. Norton & Co., 1971), p. 396.

19. Ibid., p. 391.

had not before been exercised.' "[20] Such an ambition points forward to the observation that Merleau-Ponty would make about the work of Cézanne:

> It is not enough for a painter like Cézanne, an artist, or a philosopher, to create and express an idea; they must also awaken the experience which will make their idea take root in the consciousness of others. A successful work has the strange power to teach its own lesson.[21]

The shift from physical to spiritual optics represented, then, not merely a shift in subject matter, nor even a shift, alone, in the poet's perspective on this matter. Rather it is a shift in the shaping response of the reader, a response that would "cooperate" with the work. The revolutionary aspect of Wordsworth's poetic program lies, as I shall be arguing with particular respect to "Tintern Abbey," in the very enabling process of understanding the nature of reality: in a word, his poetry constitutes a hermeneutical shift to art for *life's* sake.

Having begun my analysis of the autobiographical perspective by discussing the idealistic tendency of the self's over-projection on the world, I would like to turn now to the other side of the poet's (and the autobiographer's) problem in his or her relation with the world: namely, the problem that the *world* presents in leveling the poet's perceptions in his or her entanglement with it. Wordsworth recognizes this side of the problem when he writes in the *Preface:*

20. I am quoting here from Abrams, pp. 397–98. For the fuller context of Wordsworth's comment, see pages 426–30 in De Selincourt, *The Poetical Works of William Wordsworth,* Volume 2.
21. M. Merleau-Ponty, *Sense and Non-Sense,* trans. Hubert L. Dreyfus and Patricia Allen Dreyfus (Evanston: Northwestern University Press, 1964), p. 19.

... [A] multitude of causes, unknown to former times, are now acting with a combined force to blunt the discriminating powers of the mind, and, unfitting it for all voluntary exertion, to reduce it to a status of almost savage torpor.[22]

This "savage torpor" is no more evident than in the habits of perception that "tame the world around us by slotting everything in it to some prior generalized notions we have of things."[23] In his study of changing conceptions of reality, E. H. Gombrich refers to these habits as "mental sets" which he defines as the "attitudes and expectations ... which will influence our perceptions and make us ready to see, or hear, one thing rather than another."[24]

Given the unavoidable operation of mental set in all perceptual activity, it is hard "to disentangle what we really see from what we merely know" so that the Wordsworthian dictum of "looking steadily at the subject" was, as the poet knew, an art of the highest order. Along with the painter John Constable, Wordsworth could agree that "the art of seeing nature is a thing almost as much to be acquired as the art of reading the Egyptian hierglyphs."[25]

Looking steadily at the subject is never a simple matter of neatly separating what we see from what we know. The innocent eye, as Gombrich reminds us, is a "myth." Seeing things *as they are* is never just registering. To assume otherwise is to subscribe to what Geoffrey Hartman calls "the

22. De Selincourt, *The Poetical Works of William Wordsworth*, Volume 2, p. 389.

23. Gabriel Josipovici, *The World and the Book: A Study of Modern Fiction* (Stanford: Stanford University Press, 1971), p. 3. Josipovici is here summarizing Proust's lament about the anesthetizing effect of habit, but the lament can represent Wordsworth just as well.

24. E. H. Gombrich, *Art and Illusion: A Study in the Psychology of Pictorial Representation* (Bollingen Series XXXV, 5; Princeton: Princeton University Press, 1972), p. 186.

25. Ibid., p. 14.

dogmatic factor in realism: its assumption that a direct contact with life—with things themselves—is always available."[26]

Gombrich's own theory of perception is based on Karl Popper's distinction between a "bucket theory of the mind" where sense data are simply "deposited and processed," and a "searchlight theory" which "emphasizes the activity of the living organism that never ceases probing and testing its environment." "All cognitive processes," Popper argues,

> whether they take the form of perceiving, thinking, or recalling represent "hypotheses" which the organism sets up. . . . They require "answers" in the form of some *further* experience, answers that will either confirm or disprove them.[27]

Gombrich describes this activity as a "formula of schema and corrections." The schema are the habits of perception, the mental sets with which the artist, as a member of his or her society, necessarily begins, and which, in the process of "making and matching," he or she goes on to correct. "If seeing were a passive process," Gombrich continues,

> a registration of sense data by the retina as a photographic plate, it would be absurd for us to need a wrong schema to arrive at a correct portrait. . . . "[P]erception . . . may be regarded as primarily the modification of an anticipation." It is always an active process, conditioned by our expectations and adapted to situations. . . . We notice only when we look *for* something, and we look when our attention is aroused by some

26. Geoffrey H. Hartman, *Beyond Formalism: Literary Essays 1958–1970* (New Haven: Yale University Press, 1970), p. 62.
27. Quoted by Gombrich, *Art and Illusion*, pp. 28–29.

disequilibrium, a difference between our expectations and the incoming message.[28]

In order for new experience to be gained, it must be in dialectical relation with the experience that preceded it. On the other hand, experience must grow out of where we are and, as well, where we have been. What Hans-Georg Gadamer calls "prejudice" is, in fact, the trace that past experience has had upon us, and, like Gombrich's mental set, it inclines us toward a particular way of understanding the present. On the other hand, our prejudice must be corrected, our anticipation must be modified, since new experience necessarily fails to fit our expectations. If experience were simply continuous, repeatable, self-confirming, and unchanging, it would not be experiencable at all since we would take no notice of it. New experience is possible, then, only through "some disequilibrium" or *dislocation*.

Although "Tintern Abbey" opens on a settled and even harmonious scene, we soon learn of the "disequilibrium" that lies behind it—"the heavy and the weary weight /Of all this unintelligible world" that the poem is designed to "lighten" (ll. 39–41).[29] The word *lighten* can be taken in both of its senses: to make the "weight" less heavy, and to shed light on the meaning of such an experience. The chiaroscuro of the poem—the movement between light and dark, presence and absence, remembering and forgetting, activity and stillness, present and past—is a strategy of dialectics which keeps this basic disruption in the foreground of the poem.

We are met with a set of dialectical correspondences at

28. Ibid., p. 172.
29. This quotation and the ones following come from Wordsworth's final edition of the poem (1859–60) which appears in De Selincourt, *The Poetical Works of William Wordsworth*, Volume 2, pp. 259–63.

various levels of the poem's activity: between *kinds of seeing* (the outward eye of physical optics where there is no "interest/Unborrowed from the eye" and the inward eye of spiritual optics where "We see into the life of things"); between *modes of accessibility* (seeing and hearing in the shifts of presence and absence); and between *degrees of relatedness* (the isolation of the Hermit's cave and the poet's "lonely rooms" and what Kroeber calls the "ecological" connectedness in the "one green hue" and the "sense sublime" of deep interfusion).

The controlling dialectic of the poem is to be found, however, in the pull between the experience of locatedness and the dislocating experience of "this unintelligible world." The new-found equilibrium the poem finally achieves rests not so much on place itself ("this green pastoral landscape") as it does on the poet's mode of placing himself in relation to it. It is to be found, in other words, in the autobiographical perspective the poem enacts as it moves from the classical *topos* of the picturesque to the modern hermeneutic of landscape. As I will demonstrate, this perspective emerges from the "interfusional" structure of the poem to which the figure of Dorothy is the key.

The problem of the familiar, as I earlier suggested, is central for romanticism and, as the habits of perception that result from (and in) the leveling influence of the world, it represents the corollary to the opposing tendency towards idealism in autobiography. Just as the idealistic self might threaten to engorge the world in the direction of solipsism, the empirical world might engulf the self in the direction of positivism.

The problem of familiarity is central to autobiography as well, creating, in fact, its first obstacle: How is it possible to take notice of that to which one has become accustomed, namely, the familiarity of one's own life? As Ortega so graphically put the problem faced by the autobiographer, "those who live near a cataract do not notice its roar; it is necessary for us to put some distance between our immediate surroundings and ourselves so that they may acquire meaning in our eyes."[30]

By what means can that necessary distance be achieved? To what extreme is it necessary to go in order to see the familiar for what it is and not simply for what our habits of perception make it out to be? As with the matter of beginnings, the earlier autobiographer could more easily slip, unnoticing as it were, into a set of conventions in terms of which he could measure and align the details of his own life—in the case of an Augustine, for example, into the conventions (some would call it world view) of the classical ontology of "containment."[31]

Although there is no denying the continuing role of convention in modern autobiography, there is greater insistence on what Ortega calls man's "ontological privilege," the necessity of being the "novelist" of oneself, itself a convention in much autobiographical writing of recent times:

> I must find [the "possibilities of being"] for myself, they are not presented to me. I invent projects of being and of doing in the light of circumstance. This alone I come upon, this alone is given to me: circumstance. It is too often forgotten that man is impossible without imagination, without the capacity to invent for himself a conception of life, to "ideate" the character he is going to be. Whether he be original or plagiarist, man is the novelist of himself.[32]

30. Ortega y Gasset, *Meditations on Quixote*, p. 44.
31. See my further discussion of this notion in Chapter 5, pp. 128,131.
32. José Ortega y Gasset, "History as a System," in *History as a System and Other Essays Toward a Philosophy of History* (New York: W. W. Norton & Co., 1961), pp. 202–203.

The claiming of such a privilege can itself lead to a problem of self-accessibility as we see in the following passage from *Walden:*

> I . . . am sensible of a certain doubleness by which I can stand as remote from myself as from another. However intense my experience, I am conscious of the presence and criticism of a part of me, which, as it were, is not a part of me, but spectator, sharing no experience, but taking note of it; and that is no more I than it is you (135).

In the very act of self-reflection, Thoreau experiences only the remoteness of himself. Jacques Lacan puts the problem of the self's remoteness in this way: "I am not, wherever I am the plaything of my thought; I think of what I am whenever I don't think I am thinking."[33] One catches oneself, it would appear, only unawares.

But the problem for the autobiographer has initially to do with the fact that familiarity breeds unawareness. So close to him that he cannot see it, the autobiographer's life is simply not strange enough to be grasped. To be sure, there are always those unusual events, but the "feel" of life the autobiographer is trying to set down in writing, like Narcissus' image in the water, dissolves in the very reach for it.

There is little sign of dissolution, however, in Wordsworth's reach for the past in the first section of "Tintern Abbey." The poem opens on a scene which impresses us with its "presentness": first, with the presence of the speaker himself and the "filter" of the past he brings with him: "Five years have past; five summers, with the length/Of five long winters!" (ll. 1–2). And then with the presenting sound of the "waters, rolling from their mountain springs/With a

33. Quoted by Louis A. Renza, "The Veto of the Imagination: A Theory of Autobiography" (Ph.D. diss; Department of English, University of California at Irvine), p. 152.

soft inland murmur" that the speaker hears once again. We are present, then, at the scene's coming-to-present which is all the more firmly situated by virtue of the reiterated "once again" of the speaker's own time-line of experience.

Wordsworth's starting point in "Tintern Abbey" is the familiar—not only in his own experience of revisit both in actual fact and in the "sensations sweet" that his memory has brought back in those intervening five years, but also in the experience of many of his countrymen who, by the late eighteenth century, had made the pilgrimage to the same Abbey site in their, by now, customary search for the picturesque. In his 1770 publication of *Observations on the River Wye,* William Gilpin records his own visit to Tintern Abbey from which point one could have, he claims, the "most beautiful and picturesque view of the river."[34]

In the widely read records of his sight-seeing tours through the English countryside, Gilpin is basing his observations on a meticulous formula of the picturesque which for him had to do with the "capability" of the natural scene to resemble the Italian landscape painting that had become so fashionable in his time.[35] The influence of this school of painting was to be found everywhere in cultivated society: in the popular afternoon pastime of "viewing" scenic engravings, in landscape gardening, in poems like James Thomson's "The Seasons," and most especially in the native travel that had become a necessary substitute for the continental tours now cut off by the war in France.

34. William Gilpin, *Observations on the River Wye and Several Parts of South Wales, etc. relative chiefly to Picturesque Beauty; made in the summer of the Year 1770* (London: R. Blamire, 1779), p. 14.

35. "Capability" was the adopted name of the noted eighteenth-century landscape gardener, Lancelot Brown (1716–1783) who was often known to say to a prospective customer, "I see your park has *great capabilities.*" See John Barrell, *The Idea of Landscape and the Sense of Place 1730–1840: An Approach to the Poetry of John Clare* (Cambridge: Cambridge University Press, 1972), p. 48.

Although Gilpin starts off in his *Observations* by insisting that the rules of picturesque beauty are "not the offspring of theory" but "taken immediately from the scenes of nature, as they arise,"[36] it is clear that he, like so many of his countrymen and women, has come under the influence of what, by the 1770s, had become a mental set. From Oxford to Watney, he notes, "none of these landscapes . . . are perfect, as they want the accompaniements [*sic*] of foreground."[37] Clearly, Gilpin is making use of his notebook as the easel and brush he would otherwise employ to recompose the "canvasses" he views along the way. As he summarizes a bit later in his book,

> Nature is always great in design. She is an admirable colourist also; and harmonizes tints with infinite variety, and beauty. *But she is seldom so correct in composition, as to produce a harmonious whole.* Either the foreground, or the background, is disproportional: or some awkward line runs across the piece; or a tree is ill-placed: or a bank is formal: or something is not exactly as it should be.[38]

The "harmonious whole" that nature itself was seldom capable of producing could, for Gilpin and others, be achieved by bringing to it the "picturesque eye." As Gilpin wrote in a later set of essays, ". . . the province of the picturesque eye is to *survey nature,* not to *anatomize matter.* It throws it's [*sic*] glances around in the broad-cast stile. It comprehends an extensive tract at each sweep. It examines *parts,* but never descends to particles."[39]

36. Gilpin, *Observations on the River Wye,* pp. 1–2.
37. Ibid., p. 3.
38. Ibid., p. 31. (*Italics mine.*)
39. William Gilpin, *Three Essays: on Picturesque Beauty; on Picturesque Travel; and on Sketching Landscape: to which is added a poem, on Landscape Painting* (London: R. Blamire, 1791), p. 26.

The viewing of nature in its "sweep" was facilitated by the use of the Claude-glass, so named for the landscape painter, Claude Lorrain, whose canvasses were especially popular at the time. The Claude-glass was a black convex mirror held in such a way above one's shoulder that it could capture the reflection of the countryside just passed. The reflected composition resembled the canvasses of its name-sake: toned-down colors, prominent features stressed at the expense of detail, and panoramic.

Three things are important about the Claude-glass as it exemplifies the mode of the picturesque and thereby pro-vides a context for understanding Wordsworth's poem. First, the scene that is depicted in the glass does not arise immediately from nature, but is rather a recomposition of the natural scene. The scene in the glass is, in fact, several times removed from its original. The very act of selecting a patch of countryside as a potential "scene" removes it from its actual context, placing in the foreground certain of its elements that might otherwise go unnoticed. Putting this scene to the glass test represents still another refraction of its scenic contours.

Second, the captured scene is retrospective, the mirror reflecting from a raised prospect what occupies the space over one's shoulder in the piece of countryside one has already passed in the carriage ride. And third, the captured scene is satisfying only to the extent that it approximates a Claude painting—only, in other words, to the extent that nature imitates art.

In this case, the imitation involves a certain kind of shaping rather than the reproduction of content alone. By means of its curve, the Claude-glass will reshape the "flat-ness" of the natural scene into a "circling landscape," as the eighteenth-century poets often called it. Moreover, the am-phitheater-like scene will give the impression of great depth. As one art critic notes, "you may walk in Claude's pictures and count the miles."[40] This illusion of depth is highlighted by a combination of an elevated viewpoint and the shading of the *coulisse* that provides the framing foreground and directs the passing of the eye to the lighter horizon in the background.

All of these Claude-glass features are present in the opening section of "Tintern Abbey": the elevated viewpoint "a few miles above" the Abbey ruin from which the scene below can be commanded; the framing *coulisse* provided by the dark sycamore under which the poet reposes; the depth of focus brought into play by the "lofty cliffs" which, in painterly fashion, "connect/The landscape with the quiet of the sky." And adding to the ideality of the scene, the poet presents it as a retrospective experience or, better, as an experience whose firmness of presence is secured by the fact that it overlays a past: "again," "once again," "again," "once again"—the litany of revisit and re-cognition runs throughout the first part.

By the end of the second section, the material composition of the scene is finished. With "panoramic perception," as Albert Gérard has noted, "the poet's glance seems to encompass the whole visible world."[41] All necessary visual detail has been supplied, and the unnecessary elements, like the Abbey ruin itself, have been deleted. Individual elements —"plots of cottage-ground," "orchard-tufts," "hedge-rows," "pastoral farms," "wreaths of smoke"—have been presented in such varying degrees of clarity and muteness as to unify their impressions upon the eye in "one green hue." And what had initially been introduced as non-visual—the "Thoughts of more deep seclusion" that the cliffs "impress" —finally becomes part of the "life of things" into which the

40. Quoted by Barrell, *The Idea of Landscape*, p. 8 (see note 35).
41. Albert S. Gérard, *English Romantic Poetry: Ethos, Structure, and Symbol in Coleridge, Wordsworth, Shelley, and Keats* (Berkeley: University of California Press, 1968), p. 97.

poet is enabled to *see,* once the "eye" is "made quiet by the power/Of harmony." Were the poem to end here, as easily it could, Wordsworth would have achieved the "harmonious whole" of nature's recomposition by the picturesque eye: everything, in William Gilpin's words, would be "exactly as it should be."

But with the first word of the third and briefest section, the word *if,* the poem abruptly shifts into the conditional mood, and the "beauteous forms" of the composed scene are dissolved into "the many shapes/Of joyless daylight." Harmony may be no more than a "vain belief," the poet conjectures, at least when it is brought into proximity with the immediate reality of "the fretful stir/Unprofitable, and the fever of the world" (ll. 52–53), which Wordsworth has experienced during the five years between visits to the Abbey site. He is unable, at this midpoint in the poem, to rest easy in the composition he has managed to shape out of the scenic elements of the vista. Nor is he able to take up full occupancy in the claustral atmosphere of the "lonely rooms" of his immediate past in the city where, like the Hermit of the first section, he is but a "vagrant" dweller.

Caught between the ideal and the real, Wordsworth turns to memory, symbolized by the wanderings of the River Wye, which can transport him to the deeper resources of that earlier past "when first/I came among these hills." The lines that follow in section four about the career of Wordsworth's youthful insouciance are among the most famous in the romantic corpus, and they are usually taken as the *locus classicus* of the romantic idealization of childhood as well as the romantic nostalgia for an unmediated relation with the world.

These lines have also been widely recognized as a kind of microscosmic autobiography which present the three stages in the growth of the poet's mind that, on a larger scale, will provide the plot outline for Wordsworth's longer autobiographical account in *The Prelude*. There is first the stage of childhood immediacy when nature is "all in all." This early period of the child's oceanic feelings of union or undifferentiation is quickly followed, however, by the stage of loss. Representing the inevitable fall from thoughtless innocence into the increasingly self-conscious experience of growing up, this loss has its "abundant recompense" in the third stage of maturity when the poet learns "To look on nature, not as in the hour/Of thoughtless youth; but hearing oftentimes/The still, sad music of humanity . . ." (ll. 89–91).

In its all too smooth glide from immediacy to loss to recompense, this familiar version of the poet's story overlooks the darker aspects of the passage, the fact, for example, that Wordsworth's depiction of his carefree youthful activity—when "like a roe" he had "bounded o'er the mountains, by the sides/Of the deep rivers, and the lonely streams,/Wherever nature led," (ll. 67–70)—is quickly compared with, and seriously qualified by, an experience that derives from the poet's later years of maturity. Unselfconscious as the youthful bounding may have been, he compares it now with "a man/Flying from something that he dreads [rather] than one/Who sought the thing he loved" (ll. 70–72).

What is more, the passage illustrates as much as anything the corrosive power of time and, in a key Wordsworthian word, the "vacancy" of memory. Not only does the poet acknowledge that the time of carefree youth has passed, and gone with it the feelings of youth, "its aching joys" and "its dizzy raptures"; he has finally to conclude, "I cannot *paint*/What then I was" (ll. 75–76; *italics mine*).

These darker elements remind us once again of the dislocating experience that, as I have already suggested, motivates the poem and gives shape to its strategy of dialectics, "the heavy and the weary weight/Of all the unintelligible world." In addition to "the fretful stir/Unprofitable, and the fever of the world" that Wordsworth might classify with those general "causes . . . [that] are now acting with a combined force to blunt the discriminating powers of the mind," the weight of unintelligibility falls more personally as well on his own world. In the instance of a poet for whom recollection in tranquility is the *modus operandi* of his own poetizing, the failure of the memory to supply feelings and images represents a crisis of considerable proportions.

Such, at least, is the case for a model of intelligibility that operates on the static analogy of the *ut pictura poesis* for which, in the poem's language, there is no "interest/Unborrowed from the eye." In the realization that he is unable "to paint" that portion of his past whose lineaments are indeed inaccessible to the eye, Wordsworth recognizes the need to transcend the pictorial boundaries of the picturesque which detaches the moment from temporal flux in order to fix it once and for all. He must make the move, in other words, from physical optics to spiritual optics.

In having earlier turned to memory, Wordsworth, in fact, has already given over the reach of the eye and the spatial dimensions of the scene to the temporal dimensions within which change and even loss are inevitable. Such change and loss, however, are always part of a memory that is vital, absence and forgetting being as *real* as presence and remembering.[42] Moreover, it is precisely because the experience of change and loss are made part of the account that Wordsworth's "unpainted" portrait of his past is so vivid. Memory, after all, is an "instrument of discovery" and not an "instrument of reference."[43]

And in penetrating those deeper reaches of his past, not by way of reconstructing that past but by integrating it with

42. For the idea of "vital memory," I am indebted to Karl Kroeber, who notes, "[w]e believe in Wordsworth's memories because he does not claim that they are unchanging; they, too, are vital." See *Romantic Landscape Vision*, p. 22.

43. Samuel Beckett, *Proust* (New York: Grove Press, 1931), p. 17.

his present, Wordsworth has descended from the elevated viewpoint from which he had earlier commanded the scene below him. His viewpoint is becoming a more fully situated *stand*point which will constitute, in Ortega's words, the move from *"milieu"* to "landscape."

The density of the scene having been thickened by those earliest memories of his childhood habitation, the corrosive power of time having been acknowledged, and the "still, sad music of humanity" having been heard as a chastening "power," the poet is ready to attest to the final significance of his revisit of the Abbey site—not, as at the close of the first part of the poem, to the quiet harmony which allowed him "to see into the life of things," but to the *disturbance* which accompanies a new and more penetrating insight into the depths of life's interconnectedness:

> And I have felt
> A presence that *disturbs* me with the joy
> Of elevated thoughts; a sense sublime
> Of something far more deeply interfused,
> Whose dwelling is the light of setting suns,
> And the round ocean and the living air,
> And the blue sky, and in the mind of man:
> A motion and a spirit, that impels
> All thinking things, all objects of all thought,
> And rolls through all things (ll. 93–103; *italics mine*).

In its images of momentum—"motion," "impels," "rolls,"—this disturbing "presence" is far from being static and timeless. In the long line that reaches cosmic proportions, a line that begins with "I" and ends with "all things," we have a radical perception about the fit between the self and the cosmos—the world of conscious creatures who are aware of change and loss, as well as the world of nature. As though more firmly to anchor this large and elevated perception, Wordsworth brings it down to eye (and ear) level in the final line of the section:

> Therefore am I still
> A lover of the meadows and the woods,
> And mountains; and of all that we behold
> *From* this green earth; of all the mighty world
> Of eye, and ear. . . (ll. 103–107; *italics mine*).

The shift from the *topos* of the picturesque to the hermeneutic of landscape represents a shift from space to time or, better, to temporalized and oriented space which is *place:* "this green earth" which is no longer simply the object *of* his beholding, but rather the locus *from* which he can have access to "all the mighty world." As Merleau-Ponty finds it necessary to remind us:

> We have no way of knowing what a picture or a thing is other than by looking at them, and their *significance* is revealed only if we look at them from a certain point of view, from a certain distance and in a certain direction, in short only if we place, at the service of the spectacle, our collusion with the world.[44]

Reminders of the poet's presence at the Abbey site are supplied, to be sure, from the beginning of the poem, as I have already mentioned. But the significance of this presence—or the poet's looking at the scene before him "from a certain point of view, from a certain distance and in a certain direction"—becomes itself a matter for full attention only in the final section, where his "collusion with the world" and the interfusional structure of the poem become manifest in the figure of Dorothy.

44. M. Merleau-Ponty, *Phenomenology of Perception,* trans. Colin Smith (London: Routledge & Kegan Paul, 1962), p. 429.

In the final section of the poem, Wordsworth sees Dorothy—in her own unfolding history of union, loss and recompense—as embodying the inter-penetrative horizons of past, present, and future. The poet finds in his sister a continuity with the past which is otherwise inaccessible to him: "Oh! yet a little while/May I behold in thee what I was once . . ." (ll. 114–20). As for the future when "I should be where I no more can hear/Thy voice, nor catch from thy wild eyes these gleams/Of past existence" (ll. 147–49), he can only hope that she will continue to remember their standing together "on the banks of this delightful stream. . . ." In the final lines of the poem, there is a joining of past, present, and future when he projects his imagination of her faithful remembering:

> Nor wilt thou then forget,
> That after many wanderings, many years
> Of absence, these steep woods and lofty cliffs,
> And this green pastoral landscape, were to me
> More dear, both for themselves and for thy sake!
>   (ll. 155–59).

When Wordsworth turns to his sister in direct address in the final section, we realize that she, in fact, has been beside him from the beginning of the poem. Notwithstanding the fact that his delayed address allows the poet to end his poem on the conventionally personal note common to the period's topographical elegy to which, in many ways, "Tintern Abbey" conforms,[45] it is also the case that his turning to his sister allows him to address fully and for the first time the issues of temporality. For it is only in the interhuman world that such address is possible, the world where both the corrosive and creative powers of time are

45. See Mary Jacobus, *Tradition and Experiment in Wordsworth's Lyrical Ballads (1798)* (Oxford: Clarendon Press, 1976), p. 113.

brought into conscious awareness, where, in other words, time can become history just as space can become place. And it is here, too, in "this green pastoral landscape" of place and history that the poet's memory achieves its validation in the hope of being remembered by another. In just such hope and trust lay for Augustine the possibility for the exercise of memory, since he believed his entire life—even that portion of his infant existence before speech and consciousness—to be held in the memory of God. In his relationship with Dorothy and their shared memory of the Abbey scene, Wordsworth's collusion with the world is grounded.

The world, whose unintelligibility had set the poem in motion, has at last become truly familiar. This familiarity is not, however, a result of the poet's stamping his own image on the world, thereby transforming it into a projection of his own consciousness. The world, in fact, has resisted that picturesque design whose intelligibility resides in some harmonious and unchanging realm of "beauteous forms," an aesthetic realm which can take no account of absence, loss, or forgetting. Having achieved such a harmony by the end of section two, the poet soon acknowledges his own "sad perplexity" which becomes, a bit later, the "still, sad music of humanity." When that music finds a "dwelling-place" in Dorothy's mind, its hoped-for "sweet sounds and harmonies" leave room as well for the "solitude, or fear, or pain, or grief" that may be her "portion" as it has been the poet's.

Here again the poet turns to memory just as, in section three, he had invoked its power to explore the reaches of his earliest past. But this final invocation is to his sister's memory, not his own, and its model is not the wandering of the River Wye but his own wanderings, the memory of which will inspire, he trusts, "healing thoughts" for her.

"Nor wilt thou then forget," Wordsworth repeats. The litany of revisit and re-cognition that had secured the present's relation with the immediate past in the first section now becomes a litany that will relate a deeper past—a past that is "no more"—to their shared present, and both present and past to the future which is "not yet."

The "absent tenses," in Hannah Arendt's phrase, are gathered up in the *nunc stans* of "this green pastoral landscape," a place that has become the embodiment of time and its ambiguous powers. The scene, in other words, has become one of those "spots of time," as Wordsworth calls them in *The Prelude,* by means of which the world can be habitable. The question of habitability has been a muted theme throughout the poem, beginning with the "vagrant dwellers in the houseless woods" and the Hermit's cave at the end of the first section, the "lonely rooms" of the poet himself in the second, the cosmic "dwelling" of the "something far more deeply interfused" in section four, and finally the "mansion" and "dwelling-place" of his sister's mind in the last section.

Having removed the scene from its original context in the first sections in order to approximate the quiet harmony of a Claude painting, Wordsworth places it once again at the end of the poem. More accurately, he comes to discover the fact that the scene has its location in a world already given. The lines of accessibility to the meaning of the scene are interfused, moreover, with the "rhythmic continuity" of his own life, whose full temporality can be realized only in the *sensus communis* of shared human memory.[46] In order to

46. The phrase "rhythmic continuity" is Karl Kroeber's. Charles Altieri uses a strikingly similar phrase in describing the achievement of poems like "Tintern Abbey" which dramatize what Altieri calls "the absolute rhythms of experience." These rhythms, he writes, "are as much of the absolute as limited man can grasp, but by recognizing, for example, how development is an essentially lawful process of suffering and reconciliation, of loss and compensatory gains, one comes to trust in the recurrences informing life and to be content with what signs of the absolute he can discover. The result is not alienation but grace, the sense that man

reach this conclusion, so basic and so familiar a fact that he cannot at first attend to it, Wordsworth must come up against the world and the question of its habitability. The insufficiency he finds in the schema of the picturesque pushes him deeper into his past and finally into the imagined reaches of the future as well.

In its move from the *topos* of the picturesque to the hermeneutic of landscape, the poem finally becomes the occasion for celebrating "[o]ur cheerful faith, that all which we behold/Is full of blessings" (ll. 133–34). The unintelligibility of forgetting, loss, and even of death's "decay," continues to exert its "weight." But the "burthen of the mystery" is nonetheless "lightened," not by its removal but by its grounding in the "non-ubiquity" of the poet's life which, with its "many wanderings, many years of absence," is yet *held in place.*

That life-in-place constitutes the poet's quiet discovery of the familiar and to reach it, he has had to make the "correction" which is the title and subject of A. R. Ammons' witty poem:

> The burdens of the world
> on my back
> lighten the world
> not a wit while
> removing them greatly decreases my specific
> gravity.[47]

---

in his limited state has what may suffice for secular salvation. And the ultimate testimony of that salvation (as it was for Augustine in a different context) is that a man can both satisfactorily compose his autobiography and offer it for the enrichment of others." See "Wordsworth's 'Preface' as Literary Theory," *Criticism* XVIII (1976): 46.

47. A. R. Ammons, *The Selected Poems* (New York: W. W. Norton & Co., 1977), p. 72.

The hermeneutics of landscape allows an understanding that is a "coming to a stand,"[48] in this case, a stand that recognizes and, indeed, increases the poet's "specific gravity." Wordsworth refers to a similar experience of the familiar in Book II of *The Prelude* where, again like Augustine, he is tracing the origin of his own high calling to the prereflective period of infancy. And here, too, it should be noted, he uses the key idea of interfusion:

> Along his infant veins are interfused
> The gravitation and the filial bond
> Of nature that connect him with the world
> (ll. 242–44).[49]

Wordsworth has laid claim to his connection with the world through the adumbration of the autobiographical per-

48. Gadamer refers to Johannes Lohmann's idea of "coming to a stand" *(Zum-Stehen-Kommen)* in the former's "The Universality of the Hermeneutical Problem" (1966). To illustrate the idea, Gadamer uses the experience of finding the right word in translating a foreign language into one's own. "When we have found the right expression . . . , then it 'stands,' then something has come to a 'stand.' Once again we have a halt in the midst of the rush of the foreign language, whose endless variation makes us lose our orientation. . . . I call this experience hermeneutical, for the process we are describing is repeated continually throughout our familiar experience. There is always a world already interpreted, already organized in its basic relations, into which experience steps as something new, upsetting what has led our expectations and undergoing reorganization itself in the upheaval." See *Philosophical Hermeneutics,* trans. and ed. David Linge (Berkeley: University of California Press, 1977), p. 15.

When Wordsworth affirms "the language of the sense" as the "anchor" of his "purest thoughts," his use of the singular *sense* rather than the plural *senses* is significant. He is referring, I would argue, to the "sense sublime of something far more deeply interfused." It is this "something" that he is attempting to *translate* into "this green pastoral landscape." The hermenutic of landscape takes account of "a world already interpreted, already organized in its basic relations."

49. William Wordsworth, *The Prelude or Growth of a Poet's Mind,* ed. Ernest De Selincourt, 2d edition (Oxford: Clarendon Press, 1959), p. 54.

spective. At the same time, that adumbration is made possible by this very connection which, like the mother-child relation that is the model of his relation with nature and like the figure of the Leech-gatherer in "Resolution and Independence," is "something given," or, in the terms of the Tintern Abbey poem, "something far more deeply interfused." And while the dislocating experience of unintelligibility prepares the way for his discovery of a life-in-place, the dialectic of place and displacement makes possible as well the creation of poetry for life's sake—a poetry that will celebrate the familiar "by words/Which speak of nothing more than what we are."

4

The Autobiographical Response

THE STEREOSCOPE OF READERSHIP IN

PROUST'S *REMEMBRANCE OF THINGS PAST*

> In reality, every reader is, while he is reading,
> the reader of his own self. The writer's work is
> merely a kind of optical instrument which he
> offers to the reader to enable him to discern
> what, without the book, he would perhaps
> never have perceived in himself.
> —Marcel Proust, *The Past Recaptured*

In turning to the level of autobiographical response, I am actually returning to certain issues already introduced at the respective levels of autobiographical impulse and autobiographical perspective—namely, the issues having to do with the relation between text and life, and with the accessibility of meaning. At the level of impulse, the text-life relation is a narrative issue, while at the level of response, it is an issue more explicitly of interpretation. For autobiographical perspective, the question of access figures in the autobiographer's attempt to realize the meaning of his or her past; at this third level, that of autobiographical response, the question of access applies to the reader's attempt to appropriate the meaning of the autobiographical text.

It is at the level of autobiographical response that a reunderstanding of the autobiographical act makes its most obvious contribution to Interpretation Theory, especially in shedding light on what E. D. Hirsch has called the "validity" of interpretive activity.[1] The question of validity cannot be separated, finally, from the question of truth, and it is here, at the third level of response, that both of these questions must be addressed since it is at this level that they arise in the first place.

Not only does the angle of the autobiographical response allow me to return in new ways to old issues; it is also the angle from which I have all along been conducting my analyses of *Walden* and the two Wordsworth poems. I have wanted to show the meanings that emerge when these texts are used as occasions for a certain kind of reflection. The "horizon of expectations" set up by the autobiographical situation permitted me to "take on" these texts in order to "supply meanings" for a "need" which they themselves created within that horizon. While the term *horizon of expectations* is Karl Popper's, the other phrases come from the compelling argument Barbara Herrnstein Smith makes about the indeterminate meaning of all utterances.[2] In large part, these utterences—poems, novels, autobiographies— have value for us precisely because their meanings cannot be settled once and for all but instead require continuing interpretation.

At the same time that interpretation contributes necessary meanings to texts, it also benefits the interpreter by making accessible the value and meaning of certain experiences which, untapped, would remain hidden forever. How Professor Smith contends for what might be called the "occasionality" of meaning could just as well describe the operation of autobiographical response:

1. See E. D. Hirsch, *Validity in Interpretation* (New Haven: Yale University Press, 1963).

2. Barbara Herrnstein Smith, *On the Margins of Discourse: The Relation of Literature to Language* (Chicago: University of Chicago Press, 1978), pp. 137–54.

At every moment, throughout our lives, we are the subjects of potential "experiences," but we are not always aware of them as such. Given the practical demands of ordinary existence, we cannot give equal attention to all the events that impinge on us. . . . Our perceptions are not only directed but selected by the demands of the immediate occasion, and our experiences are usually preserved in memory only to the extent that they continue to serve our cognitive needs. Thus, much that is potentially knowable to us, because it is part of what has, in some sense, happened to us, slips by apparently unknown or at least unacknowledged.[3]

Smith goes on to argue that interpretation calls on such tacit knowledge, making it available to the knower by means of the occasion which requires him or her to acknowledge it. In effect, by rising to interpretive occasions, "we are put in full possession of what was always our property but kept in reserve, as it were, until we came of age and found some way to use it."[4]

Professor Smith makes these observations in the context of her larger quarrel with E. D. Hirsch about the "ethics of interpretation." Hirsch makes the case that interpretation is ethically constrained by the original intentions of a work's author. It is the task of interpretation, then, to reconstruct or, in Hirsch's term, to "re-cognize," those intentions by means of the "stable" concept of genre. Operating as a category of literary consciousness, genre enables the interpreter to wedge beneath the accretions of history and culture which separate him or her from the object of interpretation. While Smith allows that "there *is* an ethics of interpretation," she insists that "what it governs . . . is not the behavior

3. Ibid., pp. 144–45.
4. Ibid., p. 145.

of interpreters toward authors [as Hirsch maintains,] but rather of interpreters toward their own audiences."[5]

Whereas Hirsch locates the question of interpretation's validity in an originating situation defined in terms of authorial intention, Proust's *Remembrance of Things Past* reinforces the counterargument that Smith wants to make about the forward, not the backward, trajectory that interpretation must make: forward toward audiences, not backward toward authors. In the dimension of temporality which both inhabit, texts and lives move forward as well. Proust's narrator comes into "full possession" of who he is by rising to the interpretive occasion of the afternoon party at the end of the novel. His past becomes an "optical instrument" for reading "his own self" when he is finally able to locate himself *in front of* his life rather than returning to the magic childhood of its beginning. Even though Marcel had accepted the party invitation in the hope of being "brought nearer to [his] childhood and to the depths of [his] memory where [his] childhood dwelt," he discovers that access to those depths requires an acknowledgment of his aging and death. In this recognition of finitude, the third-person Marcel joins the first-person narrator; they, in turn, become one with the author, Marcel Proust, whose novel will celebrate this finitude.

To be sure, the confluence of protagonist, narrator, and author into a single entity supplies the most recognizable feature of any autobiography. What distinguishes *Remembrance of Things Past*, however, is the fact that these otherwise simultaneous roles of the autobiographer are kept separate until the end—an end that projects *into the future* the writing of the account we have just finished reading. These roles unite in the temporal palimpsest before which Marcel (character and narrator) finally assumes his position

5. Ibid., p. 151.

as reader and by means of which he is able to decipher the meaning of his lived past as well as to project his future vocation as an artist. The multi-dimensionality of selfhood becomes available to him, in other words, through the autobiographical response which will become (and is) the novel that *we* readers are just completing.

To accept Proust's analogy between books and optical instruments is to raise two kinds of questions for the reader. First, there are questions having to do with the instrument itself: the accuracy with which it measures and records the material under observation, the effectiveness with which it directs and holds the viewer's attention, and the authority with which it sets limits on how it may be used. Second, there are questions having to do with the quality of the view the instrument allows—with the kind of world it opens up, and with the ways it empowers the reader to inhabit that world: in Wordsworth's words, with how the work communicates to the reader the "power" to "cooperate" with *its* powers.

Matei Calinescu classifies the first set of questions as matters of "poetics," the second set as matters of "hermeneutics."[6] The former relate to the optical instrument as such and to *how* one sees; the latter relate to *what* one sees through the instrument. The autobiographical response involves both kinds of questions and activates the reciprocal relation between them. To separate them is to abstract them from the experience we actually have when we see or read something: a text, after all, is not merely a transparent window to some truth behind it, just as the surface of the present serves a more constructive purpose than simply to cover over or divert from the depth of the past. Even if it is the

6. Matei Calinescu, "Hermeneutics or Poetics," *The Journal of Religion* 59 (1979): 1–17.

case, as Calinescu says, that "books . . . are important precisely by what they show us, by what they allow us to decipher from the essential book that is in us—our true life,"[7] it is *through* and not around the instrument of the book we must go to see what we see. The instrument does more than offer an unclouded view of "our true life"; it directs, shapes, and even violates the expectations we bring to our viewing. While the book might provide an answer to the question we bring to it—in the reflective context of the autobiographical situation, for instance, the question, where does the self belong?—the book confronts us with its own question or, at the least, resists the problem-solving we demand.

It must be remembered, however, that the optical instrument of the book cannot operate independently of the reader who already inhabits a hermeneutical universe of finitude and historicity and temporality where (and *only* where) understanding takes place. That habitation is another reason why the operations of poetics and hermeneutics are always *joint* operations. Understanding is possible only at the intersection of texts and readers. Analogously, autobiographical response is possible only at the intersection of surface and depth—in the *nunc stans* where the remembered past and the anticipated future join tenses with the present.

Marcel deciphers the "essential book" in himself when he activates the reciprocity of surface and depth, of poetics and hermeneutics, from the vantage point to which the novel's final set of episodes brings him. These episodes include not only the cluster of epiphanal moments on the way to the afternoon party where so many of Proust's critics leave him; they include as well the series of recognition scenes dramatized within the "theater" of the party itself.

7. Ibid., p. 17.

The combination of these pre-party and party experiences, indeed, the juxtaposition they produce, necessitates a stereo-scopic reading on Marcel's part. By such a reading, he rises to the interpretive occasion of his "true life," even as he gets down from his "stilts" to plunge Antaeus-like "into the years." The demands of the occasion oblige him to acknowl-edge his residence in the finite world of understanding and of death—a world where meaning is always indeterminate, truth is always incarnate.

The critical literature on *Remembrance of Things Past* divides over the *"moments bienheureux"* or the epiphanies, the most famous of which is the episode of the madeleine which reconstitutes the magical world of Marcel's child-hood in Combray. As with the tasting of this little cake, these moments are initiated by a sensory stimulus—a sound, a touch, a taste—which suddenly opens a chink in the pre-sent for an upsurge of the past. The moments come always as a surprise and bring with them a feeling of well-being. In their intensity, they often seem to overcome the temporal distance between the present and the past; in their clarity, they bring a focus to the past which the passingness of present experience can never have. In fact, these moments achieve an immediacy which would seem to usurp the pre-sent altogether.

Rather than returning Marcel to something stored away in his memory and ready to be repeated, these mo-ments, Marcel believes, have their source outside of the memory altogether. They have their source in *l'oubli,* the forgotten or what the narrator calls the "involuntary mem-ory," and the epiphanal experiences that bring the past into the present have the effect of absolute originality. "It is thanks to this oblivion [*oubli*] alone," the narrator says, "that we can from time to time recover the creature that we were, range ourselves face to face with past events as that creature had to face them, suffer afresh because we are no longer ourself but he, and because he loved what leaves us now indifferent" (I, 489). Not only do the moments bring the past to a new level of clarity and intensity; it is only when the present is over and forgotten that its meaning becomes fully available to Marcel. The clearest instance of this productive delay takes place many months after the death of Marcel's grandmother when, unbuttoning his boot on the first night of his second visit to Balbec, he experiences the sensation of touch which brings back the "living reality" of his grandmother simultaneous with his first realization that she is dead.

In general, there is critical consensus as to the *nature* of these moments and to the important contribution they make to the formal organization of Proust's novel. There is fundamental disagreement, however, over their *function*. On the one side are those critics who define that function as allowing final entry into "pure time"; on the other side are the critics, far fewer in number, who view the moments as having only a provisional, not a final, function.[8] According to Dorrit Cohn, the moments are "merely the precondition—necessary, but insufficient—for creating the past through narrative."[9] For Roger Shattuck, they operate as

8. For examples of the first position, see Joseph Frank, "Spatial Form in Modern Literature," in *The Widening Gyre: Crisis and Mastery in Modern Literature* (Bloomington: Indiana University Press, 1968); Georges Poulet, *Proustian Space*, trans. Elliott Coleman (Baltimore: The Johns Hopkins University Press, 1977); Samuel Beckett, *Proust* (New York: Grove Press, 1931); and Gilles Deleuze, *Proust and Signs*, trans. Richard Howard (New York: George Braziller, 1972). For examples of the second position, see Roger Shattuck, *Proust's Binoculars* and *Marcel Proust* (New York: The Viking Press, 1974); Frank Kermode, "A Reply to Joseph Frank," *Critical Inquiry* IV (1978): 578–88; Dorrit Cohn, *Transparent Minds: Narrative Modes for Presenting Consciousness in Fiction* (Princeton: Princeton University Press, 1978); and Leo Bersani, "Proust and the Art of Incompletion," in *Aspects of Narrative*, ed. J. Hillis Miller (New York: Columbia University Press, 1971), pp. 120–42.

9. Cohn, *Transparent Minds*, p. 151 (see above).

"guide-posts which show [Marcel] the right direction without themselves taking him to his goal except by anticipation."[10]

Joseph Frank's position on the function of the moments is representative of the first set of critics who argue that they aesthetically complete Marcel's otherwise fragmentary experience and elevate it above the "mass and corporeality" of historical life. "These experiences," Frank claims, "provided [the protagonist] with a spiritual technique for transcending time, and thus enabled him to escape time's domination."[11] Using these moments as a prism, Proust's novel presents "a vision of reality refracted through an extratemporal perspective,"[12] thereby freeing his life from what Samuel Beckett calls the "intolerable limits of the real" or what Marcel himself calls at an early point in the book the "tyranny of the Particular."

As a flight from time and history, this understanding of the moments' function reverses the forward trajectory of life and turns it back to some "pure and disincarnate" set of origins. Moreover, such a disembodying approach has contributed in no small part to a general neglect of the novel's autobiographical dimensions except, in George Painter's formulation, as a Platonic "allegory" of Proust's life.[13] Frank's kind of position falls within a more widespread set of assumptions, going back as far as Plato, about the necessarily antagonistic relations between art and life. But while Plato's suspicions rested with art, whose affective powers, after all, could erode the rationality of the State, more recent suspicions rest with life, whose banality must be resisted and

10. Shattuck, *Proust's Binoculars,* p. 37 (see note 8).
11. Frank, "Spatial Form in Modern Literature," p. 20 (see note 8).
12. Ibid., p. 21.
13. George Painter, *Marcel Proust: A Biography* (New York: Random House, 1978) Vol. 1.

ultimately transcended through art.[14] This docetic understanding of the moments, as a rescue from the contamination
of time, enlists Proust's novel on the side of art against life
and represents a false separation of poetics from hermeneutics. Indeed, in sealing off the moments from the temporality
of experience, this aestheticizing approach leads only to
"hermeneutic nihilism," since they are removed from any
possibility of being understood.[15]

E. D. Hirsch's theory of "re-cognitive interpretation"
illustrates the elaborate lengths to which it is necessary to go
in order to maintain such an unnatural relation, rather *dis*-
relation, between poetics and hermeneutics. Hirsch's theory
rests on what he calls the "principle of a boundary." A
number of boundaries must be scrupulously observed if interpretation is to be valid: the boundary between the "bio-
graphical" dimension of both the author and the interpreter
and the consciously willed roles they respectively play in
specifying and uncovering the "verbal meaning" of the text;
the boundary between the "inner horizon" of the text which
constrains its unchanging "properties" and the text's "outer
horizon" which includes the "cultural and personal attitudes
the author might be expected to bring in specifying his
verbal meanings";[16] and, finally, the boundary between "interpretation" and "criticism" which must be understood, so
Hirsch argues, as fundamentally distinctive activities—the
former as attending to the "meaning" of a text, the latter to
the text's "significance":

14. See Roland Barthes on what he calls "banality anxiety," *Critical
Essays*, trans. Richard Howard (Evanston: Northwestern University
Press, 1972), p. xvi.

15. The phrase is Gadamer's in *Truth and Method*, translation edited by Garrett Barden and John Cumming (A Continuum Book; New
York: The Seabury Press, 1975).

16. Hirsch, *Validity in Interpretation*, p. 241.

The object of interpretation is textual meaning in and for itself and may be called the *meaning* of the text. The object of criticism, on the other hand, is that meaning in its bearing on something else (standards of value, present concerns, etc.), and this object may therefore be called the *significance* of the text.[17]

While significance is a changing and relative matter, meaning, Hirsch insists, is and must be "determinate." Without this core of determiniteness, the text's possible significance would have no firm ground whatsoever. The image of an iceberg illustrates for Hirsch the degree of certitude necessary to insure valid interpretation and to maintain the series of interlocking boundaries. "Inside" a boundary is reserved for "whatever is continuous with the *visible* iceberg";[18] "outside" the boundary lies whatever cannot be seen. Unlike Proust's image of the temporal palimpsest, there is no provision made for the value of "presence"—or whatever it is that lies between what is present or absent to the eye—and no recognition given to the "perceptual faith" by which we *know* that things have insides as well as outsides, backs as well as fronts, underneaths as well as aboves (which in the case of the iceberg, is most of it!), and pasts and futures as well as presents. Overlooked as well is the fact that the reputed boundaries in this theory have no existence of their own but must be *somebody's*. Boundaries, in other words, are defined and held to be legitimate by the interpreter, or the interpretive convention within which the interpreter operates, and are not simply the manifestations of a self-generating system.

Despite the fact that Hirsch's theory is designed to protect meaning from the hegemony of reader-responses, it grants a decidedly privileged position to the reader. The

17. Ibid., p. 211.
18. Ibid., p. 236.

intricate moves Hirsch prescribes and the system of checks and balances he institutes in the interest of valid interpretation tend towards what Haydon White has called a "fetishization" of reading activity, "rigidly [distinguishing] between what might be called 'master readers' and 'slave readers,' that is to say, readers endowed with the authority to dilate on the mysteries of the texts and readers lacking that authority."[19]

Like Matei Calinescu, Hirsch draws a line between poetics and hermeneutics, constructing his theory of interpretation on an objective poetics which secures meaning within the optical instrument of the text, namely, within what he calls intrinsic genre. Only when that meaning is secured can the interpreter become the hermeneutical critic who looks through the instrument to the ever-changing world where "significance" lies. Unlike Calinescu, Hirsch regards hermeneutics as not only different from poetics but as an unwelcome constraint on the procedures of verification, rather than a way of gaining access to what Calinescu calls "lived meaning."

The issue here is the accessibility of meaning. At the level of autobiographical response, the accessibility of meaning is a problem of both poetics and hermeneutics. There is no sorting out of this double operation into the clearly defined stages Hirsch's theory supposes. Such a series of discrete moves from the inner horizon of meaning to the outer horizon of significance ignores the location that the reader actually occupies. It assumes, instead, that the reader is free to move from that location with no trace of having been there at all in order to practice a "hermeneutics of the innocent eye."[20]

19. Hayden White, *Tropics of Discourse: Essays in Cultural Criticism* (Baltimore: The Johns Hopkins University Press, 1978), p. 264.
20. The phrase is Frank Lentricchia's. See "The Historicity of Frye's *Anatomy,*" *Salmagundi* 40 (1978): 103.

The problem of interpretation arising with the recent substitution of reader-hegemony for the older text-hegemony of formalism is not, as Hirsch supposes, the problem of relativism. Rather, it is the problem of absolutism or what Frank Kermode calls the "myth of transparency" and Gabriel Josipovici, the "dogma of the single vision."[21] Whatever the label, the problem of absolutism arises from the essentialist assumption that meaning resides in the text-as-such and that this meaning can be made fully visible so long as the apparatus with which it is viewed is kept in good working order. Even if such were the case, the meaning that could be certified as determinate, made fully explicit, and contained within the boundaries of conceptual coherence is already *dead* meaning, indemnified at the expense of its life in culture, or better, its life *as* culture.

A passage from *Remembrance of Things Past*—which could, in fact, be said to illumine Proust's own autobiographical theory of interpretation—exposes the inadequacy of Hirsch's scientist model of verification and raises further questions about a narrowly aesthetic definition of the epiphanal moments' function. In an earlier part of the novel, Proust has the painter Elstir offer some words of advice to the young Marcel about what counts as "evidence that we have really lived." Words about the "ultimate stage" of one's life and about the "wisdom" through which one can discover this stage furnish some ways of evaluating Marcel's state at the end of the novel. Elstir says the following:

> There is no man, . . . however wise, who has not at some period of his youth said things, or lived in a way . . . so unpleasant to him in later life that he would

21. Frank Kermode, *The Genesis of Secrecy: On the Interpretation of Narrative* (Cambridge: Harvard University Press, 1979); and Gabriel Josipovici, *The World and The Book: A Study of Modern Fiction* (Stanford University Press, 1971).

gladly, if he could, expunge it from his memory. And
yet he ought not entirely to regret it, because he cannot
be certain that he has indeed become a wise man
. . . unless he has passed through all the fatuous or
unwholesome incarnations by which that ultimate
stage must be preceded. I know that there are young
fellows . . . [who] have, perhaps, when they look back
upon their past lives, nothing to retract; they can, if
they choose, publish a signed account of everything
they have ever said or done; but they are poor creatures, feeble descendents of doctrinaires, and their wisdom is negative and sterile. We are not provided with
wisdom, we must discover it for ourselves, after a journey through a wilderness which no one else can take
for us, an effort which no one else can spare us, for our
wisdom is the point of view from which we come at
last to regard this world. . . . I can see that the picture
of what we once were, in early youth, may not be
recognisable and cannot, certainly, be pleasing to con-
template in later life. But we must not deny the truth
of it, for it is evidence that we have really lived, that it
is in accordance with the laws of life and of the mind
that we have, from the common elements of life,
. . . extracted something that goes beyond them (II.
649).

I have quoted this lengthy passage because it sets the
terms for distinguishing two kinds of autobiography as well
as for evaluating the final sections of the novel. On the one
hand, there is the account in which the autobiographer pub-
lishes, in effect, "a signed account of everything [he or she
has] ever said or done." This kind of doctrinaire autobiography would portray "successive extensions of a life laid out
along one line," as Proust says at a later point in the novel.
While the validity of this kind of account is based on the

certitude of what can be made explicit, its "wisdom," as Elstir declares, is "negative and sterile."

On the other hand, there is an account like Proust's own autobiographical novel which portrays not only the events of his life but the shifting viewpoints on these events which, according to Roger Shattuck, "assert a faith in the process of life as discovery."[22] Not simply a life copied down, this second kind of autobiography—what James Olney calls "autobiography complex" as contrasted with "autobiography simplex"—gives "evidence that [the autobiographer has] really lived," precisely because the account itself becomes an instrument of discovery and not merely a record of what "really" happened. This second kind of autobiography, Olney says, transforms the "mere fact of existence into a realized quality and a possible meaning," while the first "expresses only the self as already formed."[23] To recall the distinction that Barbara Herrnstein Smith makes about interpretation, doctrinaire autobiography "gives" a self while Proust's kind of autobiography "takes on" the self in order to find and to create the meanings necessary for real life.

The final section of *Remembrance of Things Past* begins with Marcel's return to Paris after an unspecified period at a sanatorium. As the reader is to discover along with Marcel, the time away was long enough to have brought about marked physical changes in his friends and, even more to his surprise, in Marcel himself. The episodes which form this final section cluster around the main event of the afternoon party at the Princesse de Guermantes'. These episodes divide very clearly into four parts: first, the brief description of the train ride back to Paris; second, the taxi ride to the party;

22. Shattuck, *Proust's Binoculars,* p. 116 (see note 8).
23. James Olney, *Metaphors of Self: The Meaning of Autobiography* (Princeton: Princeton University Press, 1972), p. 44.

third, Marcel's entry into the Guermantes' place of residence and his wait in the library; and fourth, the party itself.

The four sets of episodes are marked throughout by an increasingly intensified experience of change and loss which first overtakes Marcel on the train ride. He finds that his former capacity to be moved by the least incitement of his senses has been replaced by "absolute indifference." Unable to feel nature even while in the midst of it, Marcel notes of the trees he passes along the way that it is only "with boredom that my eyes register the line which separates the luminous from the shadowy side of your trunks" (II. 988). Having lost the feeling which, Rousseau-like, connects him with reality, he experiences a loss of confidence in his "talent for literature."

The change and loss that Marcel experiences as an *inner* phenomenon in the first part becomes in the second the *outer* metamorphosis which has transformed the physical appearance of Charlus, whom Marcel first sees in another cab on the latter's way to the party. The menacing *hauteur* and acute awareness of his own high station, which were signatures of an earlier Charlus, have been replaced by "an almost physical gentleness, and of detachment from the realities of life." The change has social as well as physical manifestations, as the reversal in Charlus' relationship with Mme de Sainte-Euverte tragicomically reveals. He is now the one who, at all costs, must gain recognition from her: "M. de Charlus lifted his hat, bowed, and greeted Mme de Sainte-Euverte as respectfully as if she had been the Queen of France . . ." (II. 992). The aristocratic *hubris* having been burnt out of Charlus, he has nonetheless gained the "Shakespearian majesty of a King Lear." In drawing this analogy between Charlus and the greatest of Shakespeare's aged heroes, Proust introduces a new dimension into the experience of change and loss— namely, the tragic dimension of vulnerability and death, which will be intensified and

brought directly home to Marcel at the party. In the mean-
while, the shift from the first set of episodes to the second
has upped the ante, from loss of talent to the possible loss
of life itself. Marcel's last meeting with Charlus along Guermantes' way (recalling the very different first one along
Swan's way) foreshadows the similar meetings he will have
with other figures on their way to death when he enters the
party. Between these two experiences of vulnerability and
death, however, is part three, which takes a different direction altogether.

After getting a disarmingly comic account from Jupien
on Charlus' unflagging sexual interest in young boys, Marcel continues his cab ride to the Guermantes' party. From
the moment he enters the courtyard, a dazzling series of
epiphanal moments overtakes him, one right after another.
Like the earlier episode of the madeleine, these moments are
triggered by one or another of his senses, released now from
the imprisoning indifference of the first part of this section.
The moments begin with his foot going over uneven paving
stones on the way into the courtyard. This sensation is
quickly followed by three others: his hearing a spoon against
a plate; his fingers touching a starched napkin; and his catching a distant sound of hot water pipes. Delayed until some-
what later in the library is his opening at random a copy of
George Sand's *François le Champi,* which his mother had
read to him at the beginning of the novel and from which
he now dates "the decline of my health and my will and my
renunciation." While Marcel has had similar experiences
throughout the novel, two things are different this time:
first, they have come in a cluster rather than singly; and
second, he consciously decides to analyze them during the
time he has to wait in the library for the conclusion of a
musical entertainment in the next room. The forty pages or
so that Proust gives over to Marcel's analysis, though thank-
fully briefer, are much like the extraordinarily extended

period of time (and pages) during which Marcel (as well as the reader!) was prisoner of Albertine.

Marcel's reflections on the meaning of the moments in part three read like a virtual manifesto of what I have been calling classical autobiography theory. More than any other, this section of the novel provides the basis of Gilles Deleuze's essentially Platonic reading of Proust in which Marcel's "apprenticeship to signs" unifies the novel's *recherche*. [24] According to Deleuze, the signs form a hierarchy which moves from the lowest level of what Deleuze calls "worldliness" to the highest, which is art. In the intense power of its spirituality, art transforms all the other signs by transcending their material nature and joining their meanings to an "absolute" and "original" time without a "detour" through lost time. Art transcends not only worldliness (pejoratively defined by Deleuze as the changing social world within which one is judged by *mere* appearances), but love (which *reduces* essence to existence in the particularity of the loved one), and even the epiphanal moments (which are necessarily and unfortunately *implicated* in the sensuous phenomena which triggers them). Because of their respective affiliations with the world of matter, all of these lower signs must detour through lost time in order to *mean* anything. Their meaning, then, depends on something else. "The superiority of art over life consists in this," Deleuze writes: "all the signs we meet in life are still material signs, and their meaning, since it is always in something else, is not altogether spiritual." [25] Art is the only rescue from such material contamination; what it "regains for us," according to Deleuze, "is time as it is coiled within essence, as it is born in the world enveloped by essence, identical to eternity." [26]

24. Deleuze, *Proust and Signs* (see note 8).
25. Ibid., p. 41.
26. Ibid., p. 46.

There is much in Marcel's analysis of the moments which lends support to the essentialist ontology influencing Deleuze's reading and informing that autobiography theory which locates the true self outside of time and change (and death) in the realm of absolute essence. The moments make possible, we are told, a resurrection of the "true self" by creating "the man freed from [the] order of time." As *interior* experiences creative of selfhood, the moments put Marcel in touch with the reality beyond time and death even though that contact cannot resist the "inertia" of matter for very long. As a bridge between the finite and the eternal, the moments have a metaphorical function much like art, which converts matter to spirit and which unites sensation and memory, thereby liberating the artist from the "contingencies of time."

Marcel's dilation on the aesthetic function of the moments defends against the vulnerability which the appearance of Charlus has introduced and which up-coming scenes at the party will intensify. What seems to be promoted by Marcel's analysis, as well as by the autobiography theory I have been challenging, can be understood, in fact, as a "doctrine of *in*vulnerability." Ascribed by Hannah Arendt to the Greek Stoics (who were among the first, she claims, to have "discovered" the interiority of the self), this doctrine allows one to withdraw from the world while in the midst of it.[27] Withdrawal offers a way of mastering the world by refusing to consent to its reality and, instead, creating an interior world which is superior to the other in every respect except in its reality quotient. The motto of this doctrine, Arendt suggests, would read like this: "Be stonelike and you will be

27. Hannah Arendt, *The Life of the Mind: Willing* (Harcourt Brace Jovanovich, 1978), pp. 73–84. Arendt introduces the doctrine in the context of her remarks on the omnipotence of the will. "Underlying all the arguments for such omnipotence is the matter-of-course assumption that reality *for me* gets its realness from my consent . . ." pp. 81–82.

invulnerable. *Ataraxia,* invulnerability, is all you need in order to feel free once you have discovered that reality itself depends on your consent to recognize it as such."[28] Marcel reveals something like this stonelike attitude when he theorizes that the people once most dear to him, including above all his now-dead grandmother, served no greater function than to "pose for him like models for a painter." Such "posthumous infidelity," as he understatedly recognizes this attitude to be, reveals nothing so much as the delusional and defensive lengths to which the imperialistic self is forced to go to fend off the threatening knowledge of its and others' finitude.

Were the novel to have ended in the library, one might conclude (recalling William Gilpin's words on the harmony achieved by the picturesque eye) that everything was "exactly as it should be," at least according to Deleuze's reading. Part three, however, gives way to the fourth and final part of the novel when, in the midst of Marcel's determination to go on with his literary career, he finds himself "suddenly in the main drawing room, in the middle of a party which . . . was to seem very different from those I had attended in the past, and was to assume a special character in my eyes and take on a novel significance" (1. 1039). The significance of the party will, indeed, be novel: it will be here, in the context of life's trajectory toward death (the ultimate experience of change and loss), that the real test of the moments will come and here, too, that Marcel will discover the truth of selfhood. He will make this two-fold discovery (of the synechdochical, not the metaphorical, value of the moments and, correspondingly, of the multidimensionality of selfhood) not in an interior set of private sensations which delivers him from the contingencies of time, but in a *social* experience which plunges him into the "mighty dimension of

28. Ibid., p. 79.

Time" and allows him to come out from behind his life, as it were, and to view it from the outside in, not the inside out.

The series of temporal "portraits" that Marcel will find in front of him will serve, finally, to rehabilitate the *value of the surface*—the surface which heretofore had operated, at best, as no more than a vehicle to a more essential reality beyond it and, at worst, as no better than an obstacle which restrained or repulsed any further search. In either case, the surface was subject to devaluation as a result of what Roger Shattuck diagnoses as Marcel's "metaphysical envy" for what always and illusively lay behind or beneath that surface.[29] Paul Ricoeur defines this attitude as the "category of the *Pseudo*" and identifies it with "the evil infinite of human desire—always something else, always something more—which . . . *seems* to constitute the reality of man."[30] Surface will have value when Marcel's autobiographical response allows him to acknowledge and to appropriate the reality of his life as really lived. The party, in effect, takes him back once again to Plato's cave, this time to discover reality *in* appearance and not behind or above it: the bona fide "hieroglyph of life" resides in change, not permanence, and in a worldliness which is far more real than the spirituality of supra-worldly essences.

Finding himself at last in the drawing room, Marcel is immediately struck by the disguises which seem to mask the true identity of all the guests. Almost all of them, for example, have put on "a powdered wig." His host, the Prince de Guermantes, has gone even further with his get-up: to the wig he had added "a white beard and [he] dragged his feet along the ground as though they were weighed with soles of lead, so that he gave the impression of trying to impersonate one of the 'Ages of Man' " (ii. 1039). One after another,

29. Shattuck, *Proust's Binoculars*, p. 39 (see note 8).
30. Paul Ricoeur, *The Symbolism of Evil*, trans. Emerson Buchanan (Boston: Beacon Press, 1969), p. 254.

these figures present themselves before Marcel's eyes. In much the way the impressionist painter Elstir captured the visual immediacy of the seascape on his canvasses, Proust, too, captures the brilliance of sheer surface in his Dantesque presentation of the figures Marcel sees in the drawing room. Particularly impressive is a group scene like the following —a sharply etched tableaux which translates what might just as well be a Gustave Doré illustration of *The Inferno* into narrative surface:

> Some men walked with a limp, and one was aware that this was the result not of a motor accident but of a first stroke: they had already, as the saying is, one foot in the grave. There were women too whose graves were waiting open to receive them: half-paralyzed, they could not quite disentangle their dress from the tombstone in which it had got stuck, so that they were unable to stand up straight but remained bent towards the ground, their head lowered, in a curve which seemed an apt symbol of their own position on the trajectory from life to death, with the final vertical plunge not far away (II. 1053).

The figures gathered together at the party offer what Marcel calls "a peepshow of the years, the vision not of a moment but of a person situated in the distorting perspective of Time" (l. 1043). To recognize them, he must readjust his own vision and adopt what Paul Ricoeur calls "metaphorical seeing," but what I would call *synechdochical* seeing —the seeing of a quality in time, not an image in space: "a stereoscopic vision," says Ricoeur, "in which the new situation is perceived only in the depths of the situation disrupted by the category mistake."[31] Marcel must translate the category mistake of presumed disguise into the new reality of an aging Prince. He must, in effect, look twice. Moreover, he must look at himself a second time when he is shocked into the realization that the young men with whom he continues to identify himself now view him as "an old gentleman."

But the most basic mistake he must correct in view of this new situation has to do with the category of space within which Marcel had earlier assumed the epiphanal moments to have arrested time. Having decided in the library that these moments could be used in the service of an art that would transcend the contingencies of time, Marcel, now confronted with contradictory evidence, must look again. As he says, "I had made the discovery of this destructive action of Time at the very moment when I had conceived the ambition to make visible, to intellectualize in a work of art, realities that were outside Time" (II. 1046–47).

The notion of the stereoscope is central to Roger Shattuck's reading of Proust in *Proust's Binoculars.* [32] According to that reading, Marcel finally rejects the "faulty optics" of the moments—an optics based on "a single *instantané*"—in order to account for the phenomena of aging and death with which he is confronted at the party. The experience of aging and imminent death compels him to adopt the "stereoscopic principle" of the "double take" which, for Shattuck, represents the "true optics of Time" that gives Marcel "an accurate and lasting image in depth."

In order to be released from the faulty optics of the epiphanal moments and to discover the true optics of time, Marcel must acknowledge the reality of death—not only the death of the aging friends around him at the party, but his own mortality as well. In acknowledging his mortality, he

leen McLaughlin and John Costello (Toronto: University of Toronto Press, 1967), p. 231.

32. Shattuck, *Proust's Binoculars,* pp. 42–46 (see note 8).

can also affirm his residence in the "mighty dimension of Time," the "dimension in which life is lived" (II. 1127). Time is also the dimension of *presence* in which the "stages" between the present and the past have their virtual life, making it possible for Marcel to connect, for example, the "massive white-haired lady making her way through the room with elephantine tread" to the "fair-haired girl, the marvellous waltzer, whom I had known in the past" (II. 1054). Instead of a "sequence of juxtaposed but distinct 'I's' which could die one after the other or even come to life eternally" (II. 1047), this snapshot view of selfhood can give way to a multidimensional understanding of the self's temporal depth.

The newly won perceptual faith which makes it possible for Marcel to experience so compellingly the virtual dimension of time is empowered by the liberating experience of otherness he has when he looks into the eyes of his aging friends. In those eyes he finds "the first truthful mirror [he has] ever encountered." What he sees in those eyes is not a reflection of himself, but rather a new illumination about how important it is *to be seen.* He sees himself being seen, not a direct reflection of himself. And how he is seen has everything to do with who he is. In Georges Gusdorf's contrast between biography and what he assumes to be the greater truth of autobiography, he dismisses the former as simply a record of how the person *appears* from the outside rather than a true account which can come only from the autobiographer's "inside."[33] The following passage suggests, however, that the self's appearing has the greater priority, since it is only in such appearing that the self can receive the "answering looks" which confirm its reality and reveal its truth:

33. See note 11, Chapter 1.

I was able to see myself, as though in the first truthful mirror which I had ever encountered, reflected in the eyes of old people, still young in their own opinion as I in mine, who when I spoke of "an old man like myself" in the hope of being contradicted, showed in their answering looks . . . not a glimmer of protest (II. 1046).

The ultimate significance of the party could be said to lie in the combination of several things: its enjoining on Marcel an acknowledgment of his mortality and thereby of his fully dimensional residence in time; its rehabilitation of the value of the surface by means of the narrative contextualizing and temporalizing of the epiphanal moments; and, in the recognition of the enlivening reality of others as the *sine qua non* of selfhood, its enabling Marcel—main character, narrator, *and* author—to become the *biographer* of the self to which he can now lay claim in autobiographical response.

Proust's autobiographical novel demonstrates how depth can be appropriated: not by invasive diving for deep structures, not by an aesthetic catapult out of contaminated time *(temps perdu)* for the recovery of pure original time, but by a productive reading of surface which, conducted from within the multidimensionality of time, is what I am calling the autobiographical response. If the autobiographical impulse establishes the dehiscence of time—the fact that depth exists in anticipation of becoming surface—then the autobiographical response testifies to the fact that the self can exist in the temporality of depth only when it is "read" by others, only when it is *taken to be what it is* and not when it simply "is" in isolation from the world. The *I* exists only in the context of the *we;* selfhood is a plural, not a singular, concept. Moreover, the self exists only as a changing and finite creature, only as a creature who loses and forgets as well as one who finds and remembers, only as a *vulnerable* creature who, as Proust concludes, must get off his "living stilts" to plunge Antaeus-like into the "years." As Maynard Mack said at the end of his wonderful book on *King Lear:* "When we come crying hither, we bring with us the badge of all our misery; but it is also the badge of the vulnerabilities that give us access to whatever grandeur we achieve."[34] Marcel and the reader must learn the lesson of Charlus.

"The only true voyage of discovery," Proust wrote in an early section of *Remembrance of Things Past,* ". . . would be not to visit strange lands but to possess other eyes, to behold the universe through the eyes of another." Our reading of works like Proust's might be said to provide just such a voyage of discovery, a way of looking at the universe of our common experience from a perspective other than our own. Thoreau was referring to a similar alteration of the reader's perspective when he asked in *Walden,* "could a greater miracle take place than for us to look through each others' eyes for an instant?" The test of serious reading depends on the extent to which our customary habits of response are disturbed. In this respect, reading has the important function of clearing out the underbrush of accepted tradition in order to make way for new values and, in the case of autobiography, for new images of the self. Reading, then, has a *critical* function—the function of what Ricoeur calls distantiation.

At the same time, Proust makes a counter-claim when he suggests that a book provide the occasion for the self-reading of the reader. Instead of distancing the reader from his or her knowledge of selfhood, the book is an optical instrument which enables the reader to participate in that

34. Maynard Mack, *King Lear in Our Time* (Berkeley: University of California Press, 1965), p. 117.

knowledge at a deeper level. While the first kind of reading fulfills the function of poetics, the second kind fulfills the function of hermeneutics. According to Hans-Georg Gadamer, the "nature of the hermeneutical experience is not that something is outside and deserves admission. Rather, we are possessed by something and precisely by means of it we are opened up for the new, the different, the true."[35] While the poetics of reading is made possible through distantiation, the hermeneutics of reading depends on participation in order to achieve what Ricoeur calls the "consciousness of belonging."[36]

Proust's novel combines these ways of reading; it furnishes both a poetics which enables Marcel to read the "text" of his life "through the eyes of another," and a hermeneutics which makes it possible for him to become a "reader of his own self." The autobiographical response provides a context within which the elements of poetics and hermeneutics, held often to be taxonomically distinct, are brought into new relation. What mediates between the two is the stereoscope of readership.

Marcel must "re-author" the book of life he has lived before it can be the optical instrument by means of which he can become the reader of himself. The depth of his past is recoverable only through the shimmering surface of the present he finds displayed in all its fading, but often comic, grandeur at the afternoon party of the Princesse de Guermantes. Marcel finds at the party, in all the disguised characters whom he must recognize as the aging friends from whom he has been separated, the truthful mirror of selfhood. What he discovers is not the classical autobiographical self

35. Hans-Georg Gadamer, "The Universality of the Hermeneutical Problem," in *Philosophical Hermeneutics,* trans. and ed. David Linge (Berkeley: University of California Press, 1977), p. 9.
36. Paul Ricoeur, "Ethics and Culture: Habermas and Gadamer in Dialogue," *Philosophy Today* XVII (1973): 157.

which reflexively and singularly resides on the other side of the mirror. Rather, he discovers the reflection of who he is in the answering looks which *correct* his mistaken view of himself as the young man of the past. The process of time and aging which takes palpable form in the tableaux before him enacts a temporal palimpsest which fills in the empty space between past and present and which connects the past and present with the future Marcel will have as the writer, Marcel Proust. The book he will write takes momentum from the acknowledgment he can now make of his vulnerability as a finite creature.

That book, of course, is the autobiographical novel the reader is just finishing as well as the book he or she must re-author in rising to the interpretive occasion it requires. The autobiographer of this novel—as main character, narrator, and finally, too, as author—has set out for the reader the path towards yet another autobiographical response.

5

The Worldliness of Autobiography

AUGUSTINE'S *CONFESSIONS,*

BLACK ELK SPEAKS, AND

THE *CREDO UT INTELLIGAM*

> Beliefs constitute the basic stratum, that which
> lies deepest, in the architecture of our life. By
> them we live, and by the same token we rarely
> think of them.
> —José Ortega y Gasset, "History as a
> System"

The autobiographical situation makes it possible
to account for autobiography as a significant human and
cultural activity as well as to re-instate its membership in the
category of life. That membership must be cancelled when
selfhood is circumscribed by textuality or when alienation
is taken to be the inevitable price of bringing the self to
language. In opposing both of these contentions, I have
argued that the *autos* of autobiography cannot be realized in
disjunction from its *bios* and, further, that the relation between *autos* and *bios* is enacted, not sabotaged by, language
or the *graphie* of autobiography. The ecological relation
among these elements empowers the genre of autobiography, a dynamic finally unconstrained, though shaped, by the
text.

The *autos, bios,* and *graphie* of the genre have their
respective counterparts in the perspective, impulse, and re-

Eakin

sponse which constitute the autobiographical situation—the hermeneutic universe in which all understanding takes place. Autobiography can be said to model the interpretive activity that makes understanding possible and that marks our common humanity. As such a model, the problem of autobiography must be repositioned from a problem *before* the fact to a problem *after* the fact: from the question of whether or not the self can make the move from inside to outside, from private to public, from silence to speech without sacrificing its essential integrity, to the fact that "my life succeed[s] in drawing itself together in order to project itself in words, intentions, acts."[1] It is the *success* of autobiography, not its failure, that becomes the problem—one of over-orientation rather than alienation, of completing not losing the self, of regressing to what Frank Kermode has called "paradigmatic rigidity."[2]

In other words, the problem of autobiography lies in the threat of ideology which dogs all narrative in its compulsion toward wholes. The pull toward ideology is all the more difficult for autobiography to resist because the ideological impulse has so much in common with the autobio-

1. What I am defining as the problem of autobiography is only one aspect of what Merleau-Ponty calls the "problem of rationality" about which he writes: "But, it will be asked, if the unity of the world is not based on that of consciousness, and if the world is not the outcome of a constituting effort, how does it come about that appearances accord with each other and group themselves together into things, ideas and truths? And why do our random thoughts, the events of our life and those of collective history, at least at certain times assume common significance and direction, and allow themselves to be subsumed under one idea? Why does my life succeed in drawing itself together in order to project itself in words, intentions and acts? This is the problem of rationality." See *Phenomenology of Perception,* trans. Colin Smith (London: Routledge & Kegan Paul, 1962), p. 408. Merleau-Ponty addresses this problem through his notion of "being in the world." Hannah Arendt addresses the same problem through her notion of "worldliness"—a term which I am using in this chapter to characterize *true* autobiography.

2. See note 11, Chapter 2.

graphical impulse. Both arise from a simultaneous ground-edness and a need for acknowledging a meaningful orientation in a world; both are responses to the finitude and vulnerability that characterize the human condition; and both represent an effort to take hold of something in the process of vanishing or disintegrating. Moreover, both impulses function toward the end that Clifford Geertz ascribes to ideology: "to render otherwise incomprehensive . . . situations meaningful, to so construe them as to make it possible to act purposefully within them."[3]

Autobiography can exhibit a compulsion toward wholes in two ways: either by assuming an Eleatic definition of the self as an already complete entity which simply unfolds, acorn-to-oak fashion, in the autobiographical process; or by aiming towards an idealized selfhood, freed from the contingencies of historical time and space, and finally coming to rest in transcendental repose. Autobiography becomes ideology when its *autos* comes to completion as a being-in-itself, when the multidimensionality of lived meaning, with its inescapable burden of unintelligibility, is abandoned for the unambiguous clarity of monochromatic truth. Self has been won but sealed off from the theatre of "world-liness" where, by appearing to and experiencing the display of other selves, it *real*izes itself. Shielded from any intimations of mortality, the self has simply been removed altogether from experience.

While this account of the ideological impulse comes close to caricature if not pathology, something approximating this solipsistic version of selfhood can be recognized in a certain way of reading Augustine's *Confessions*. This way of reading the *Confessions* has contributed in no small part to the essentialist tradition of classical autobiographical the-

3. Clifford Geertz, *The Interpretation of Cultures: Selected Essays* (New York: Basic Books, 1973), p. 220.

ory, not only because of the additional weight of presumably religious appeals, but also because this text—taken by many to be the first specimen of the autobiographic genre—occupies so secure a place in the autobiographical tradition as to be a touchstone in the very definition of the genre.[4] Although I do not want to question its normative status, I do want to reexamine the assumed grounds of the *Confessions'* place in the tradition, since these grounds continue so basically to guide or, rather, to misguide current thinking about the religious significance of autobiography. Since its security in the tradition has bred a certain familiarity which makes reexamination difficult, some way must be found to defamiliarize the text, some way to experience the strangeness of its questions instead of the obviousness of its answers.

As I have defined it, the autobiographical situation establishes the direction needed to take up the questions of the *Confessions,* as well as provides the distance required to evaluate the autobiographical status of the text. Looking at the questions of the text as if they were yet unsolved, we might not so easily assume that the religious significance of the work depends somehow upon divine rescue from a time-bound and materially contaminated existence in order to achieve an eternal and otherworldly wisdom. Were this the case, autobiography would become no more than the bridge Augustine burns behind him, once his true self passes over the threshold to an atemporal repose. If this view is correct,

---

4. I have in mind what I call the "gnostic" interpretation given the *Confessions* by such critics as Eugene Vance ("Augustine's *Confessions* and the Grammar of Selfhood," *Genre* VI [1973]: 1–28) and, more recently, William C. Spengemann in *The Forms of Autobiography: Episodes in the History of a Literary Genre* (New Haven: Yale University Press, 1980). Both readings detemporalize and aestheticize the *Confessions* in order to fit it into the critics' respective systems: for Vance, into a reified textual system he calls the "*logos* of the Word"; for Spengemann, into a "poetic" mode which allows the self a "direct, vertical relation to the absolute truth."

one would do well to cancel the *Confessions'* long-standing membership in the autobiographical tradition, since the first-person narrative has necessarily to be aborted to accommodate a third-person and worldless knowledge of God. Cut off from the vital momentum of temporality, the work would thereby give birth to an undeveloped and lifeless self. Or to put the matter still another way, the life that was saved would not be Augustine's own.

When the *Confessions* is viewed through the lens of the autobiographical situation, it discloses the hermeneutic at the very heart of autobiography—namely, the religious hermeneutic of *credo ut intelligam* that informs and is enacted by the genre, securing its meaning within and not outside the world of lived experience. The *Confessions* requires no passport to eternity, no extraterritorial rights beyond time, in order to gain religious significance either for its present readers or for Augustine as a "reader" of his life. The act of autobiography is finally to be understood as moving more deeply into time, not beyond it—in Augustine's words, a presenting of "man in his deep"; in Hannah Arendt's terms, a securing of the *worldliness* of belief.

Two issues figure centrally in my reexamination of the *Confessions*, the one having to do with the autobiographical status of the text, the other with the proper grounds upon which we can accept this or any work as religious autobiography. Relevant to both issues is the relation of discourses in the *Confessions*—in particular, the relation of the analytic and exegetical portions in Books Ten through Thirteen to the narrative section in the first nine books. Roy Pascal, among others, dismisses the final books as no more than a long philosophical footnote on the "autobiography proper" of the first nine. Even Peter Brown tends to set off these last books from the rest when he writes that "the remaining three books of the *Confessions* are a fitting ending to the self-revelation of such a man: like a soft light creeping back over a rain-soaked landscape. . . ."[5]

I would argue, however, that these last books, along with earlier passages that Pascal dismisses as "interjectory," are themselves parts of the autobiographical "landscape." Indeed, these books and passages are at the center of the landscape, for it is most especially in them that one finds Augustine's efforts to situate both the confessing "I" and the God to whom he is confessing.

The notion of placement, along with the corollary question of location, is operative throughout the *Confessions.* This notion serves not only to relate the work's variety of discourses, but it secures the autobiographical status and, finally, constitutes the religious significance of the *Confessions,* when placement or situatedness or location are understood in the operative terms of the *credo ut intelligam.* The hermeneutical principle of "believing in order to understand," which Augustine will make explicit in his later writings on the Gospel of John, is already implicit in the *Confessions.* The "I" that confesses is the "I" that lives and has its life in believing. *Believing* and *living:* these words share a common set of roots; both of them participate in the idea of being "sticky," of adhering, remaining, and especially of staying alive or, more simply, of living.[6] The primary feature in this catalogue of etymological associations is the idea of locatedness. Both life and belief involve adherence— not, however, as an assent to universal principles or doctrinal formulations *sub specie aeternitatis,* but as anchorage

5. Peter Brown, *Augustine of Hippo: A Biography* (Berkeley: University of California Press, 1967), p. 180.

6. See Eric Partridge on "life," *Origins: A Short Etymological Dictionary of Modern English* (New York: Macmillan Publishing Co., 1977), p. 353.

in the particular circumstances of one's temporal existence.

Far from being "stuck" by the fact of locatedness, it is only in the acknowledgment of such anchorage that one is able to move forward. In Gadamer's terms, our finitude is our mode of access to reality; or as Ortega y Gasset might put it, "Man cannot live in radical uncertainty about himself and every one of his circumstances. . . . [E]very life has some certainty."[7] Such certainty is a "certainty of faith": a "zone of stability" or a "*creencia.*"

Creencias are culturally operative convictions about the way reality is put together and how, as a consequence, human beings ought to behave. In *The Modern Theme*, Ortega defines *creencias* as the "nets, provided with meshes of definite sizes and shapes which enable . . . [people] to achieve a strict affinity with some truths and to be incorrigibly inept for the assimilation of others."[8] These nets become visible only when their "meshes" are strained by unexpected events, by experience that can no longer be made sense of through the "sizes and shapes" of their particular grids. As the literature of theodicy so amply illustrates, the "design" of the universe comes under question, or even into the field of our attention, only when the experience of suffering and evil puts it to the test. In this respect, one comes to an *awareness* of Paradise only when it is lost.

Whether or not we want to subscribe to some Miltonic doctrine of the fortunate fall, it is true to say that experience, either personal or cultural, is available to us *as our own* only when our firm assumptions about reality are unhinged by

7. Karl J. Weintraub, *Visions of Culture: Voltaire, Guizot, Burckhardt, Lamprecht, Huizinga, Ortega y Gasset* (Chicago: University of Chicago Press, 1969), p. 261. The words are Weintraub's, but they might well have been those of Ortega himself, so close are they to the spirit of the latter's meaning and tone.

8. José Ortega y Gasset, *The Modern Theme*, trans. James Cleugh (New York: Harper and Row, 1961), p. 89.

our coming up against the unexpected and the unintelligible. At the same time, we would be unable to "catch" any experience at all, old or new, without the assumptive reality of our nets. As E. H. Gombrich has suggested, we need "schema" in order to "correct" them.

The Augustinian *credo ut intelligam* testifies to the fact that there is always a *place* from which the autobiographer adumbrates his or her perspective on the self. (Perspective, moreover, is an organizing, not a deforming, of reality.) This place derives from the circumstances of the autobiographer's past—not alone the "raw data" of those circumstances, but the net of *creencias* by means of which those data have been contoured into the transpersonal or cultural meanings that make them available to the experiencing self. Augustine's "I believe" does not remove him to some atemporal space where the tenses of his cultural existence are translated into God's "eternal To-day." The belief that leads to his own autobiographical understanding of his life-in-God represents an acknowledgment of the trust he can have in his own temporal existence as a vehicle of meaning.

To define *credo* as such an acknowledgment is not to say that Augustine was captive to the nets of orthodoxy which helped him to shape the meaning of his own experience. Nor is it to say that his experience was available to him as unmediated by any grids of significance whatsoever. It is rather to say that the autobiographical situation of the *Confessions* is comprised not alone by the narrative account of the first nine books where Augustine adumbrates a perspective on his past from the standpoint his conversion provides. It is comprised as well by the opening prayer and the later books which frame and respond to that account, grounding its perspective and securing its standpoint in the reality of Augustine's life as lived. To use the words of Michael Polanyi, Augustine's "believing is conditioned at its source by [his] belonging"[9]—by (to use yet another word, this one Hannah Arendt's) the fact of his *worldliness*.

Augustine's own theory of interpretation as he employs it in his reading of *Genesis* in the final books of the *Confessions* provides the larger theoretical context for understanding the relation of discourses. "Take up and read": Augustine is acting once again on the child's admonition that figured in the conversion experience he recorded in Book Nine. He is turning now to the problem of origin, a problem that is not, after all, unrelated to the problem of autobiography, but this time as it is illumined in the Old Testament account of the creation. Although he wants to get his mind around the baffling notion of creation *ex nihilo* and how to imagine himself back to a time before time, Augustine's first problem is how to *read* the account before him. From the principles of interpretation he incorporates in his reading of the Scriptures, one can get a firmer grasp on the "reading" he does of his own life.

As is the case in Augustine's "life-reading" act of autobiography, the concept of placement is central to a truthful understanding, here of the Scriptures. It figures in his theory of interpretation in three ways: (1) Authorial intention is determined by the reader's imagining himself in the author's—in this case, Moses'—place: ". . . I cannot believe that Thou gavest a less gift to Moses . . . than I would wish or desire Thee to have given to me, had I been born in the time he was, and hadst Thou set me that office. . . ."[10] But even in the assurance that one can expect no less of Moses

9. Michael Polanyi, *Personal Knowledge: Towards a Post-Critical Philosophy* (Chicago: University of Chicago Press, 1974), p. 322.
10. Augustine, Bishop of Hippo, *The Confessions of Saint Augustine*, trans. E. B. Pusey, p. 300. Subsequent citations will be indicated by page numbers directly following the quotations in my text.

than one would of oneself under the same circumstances, there is no restricting the truth of the passage at issue to one thing. (2) Recognizing the pluralism of truth, Augustine's theory of interpretation takes the reader's own placement seriously in defining the truth of the text: ". . . every man may draw out for himself such truth as he can upon these subjects, one, one truth, another, another, by larger circumlocutions of discourse" (301). So long as the context of interpretation is defined by the situation the reader's life actually occupies, his or her "horizon" contributes to, rather than deflects from, a truthful understanding of the text's meaning. (3) Finally, there is the matter of Augustine's own placement before the text he wants to understand. Far from dismissing the "origins of self" for the "origins of the universe," as one critic wants to argue, Augustine's reading of *Genesis* has everything to do with his own life as lived and now confessed.[11] In placing *himself* before the Scriptures, he brings with him his lifelong interest in language and speech as well as the larger question of location that impels his autobiographical activity throughout the thirteen books. When some critics suppose that Augustine's conversion represents a mere transference of loyalty from Mother Monica to Mother Church, they are wrong only in imagining it could be otherwise. Augustine does not jump out of his skin to be converted. The life that is converted is the life he has lived, even a life of attachment—some would say an unnatural attachment—to his mother. And in being turned around to himself, he is turned to the God who has upheld that life all along.

The *Confessions* opens with one of the many impassioned prayers that will lace the entire work. This first one

11. Vance, "Augustine's *Confessions* and the Grammar of Selfhood," p. 17 (see note 4).

introduces the motifs that will concern Augustine throughout the work:

> And how shall I call upon my God and Lord, since,
> when I call for Him, I shall be calling Him to myself?
> and what room is there within me, whither my God
> can come into me? whither can God come into me,
> God who made heaven and earth? is there, indeed, O
> Lord my God, aught in me that can contain Thee? (1).

The self making "room" for God, God making
"room" for the self—the questions continue, all of them
dealing with the idea of containment and the location of
God and self. Since God made heaven and earth, do they not
therefore contain Him? And since he, Augustine exists, does
he not already contain God, because without containing
God, he would have no existence? Or is it rather the case
that it is God Himself who is the container "since what
Thou fillest Thou fillest by containing it?" If God were the
contained and not the container, He would have been
poured out when the vessel of creation was broken.

Having momentarily reached the conclusion that God
must be the container of His creation at the same time as He
is contained by it, Augustine is led to another series of
speculations: Since creation cannot be exhaustive of God's
being, does creation then contain only a part of Him? If only
a part, which part? And do the different orders of creation
contain "all at once the same part? or each its own part, the
greater more, the smaller less?" (3). As he later and half-
humorously views the matter in Book Seven, an elephant
might have more of God than a sparrow.

Augustine will eventually realize that no answer to
these questions is possible so long as he continues to measure
God's being as though it were corporeal matter. In fact, he
will come to see that questions about God are, in truth,

questions about the self and the self's actual experience. The clue to God lies in the fact of his own life, and this fact, not God, is the true mystery. "But where was I, when I was seeking Thee?" he asks in Book Five, "And Thou were before me, but I had gone away from Thee; nor did I find myself, how much less Thee!" (73–74). And even after his conversion, he can admit in Book Ten, ". . . I know less of myself than of Thee. I beseech now, O my God, discover to me myself. . ." (244). Once Augustine locates himself in his own life, he will have located God who, of course, has been there all along. Something of this understanding operates towards the end of the opening prayer when Augustine concludes his long series of questions and answers with yet another question: ". . . who is God save *our* God?" (3; *italics mine*).

Augustine began the writing of his *Confessions* in A.D. 397, about a decade after his conversion. From the perspective of that conversion, he turns the spotlight on his past life in the first nine books whose narrative begins with his infancy and ends with the death of Monica. He finds no moment free of sin in that spotlight, even the playful moments of his boyhood, because the direction of his life was other than towards the God he now confesses as sovereign. His life before conversion was misdirected; it was a life lacking true orientation, a life whose vagrancy led him as far from himself as it did from God.

Augustine's questioning, however, does not end with the *metanoia* of Book Nine. With as much urgency as one finds in the opening prayer, he turns once again in Book Ten to the question of location. In the books that follow the account of his conversion, Augustine is in the process of more explicitly bringing himself up-to-date in that "middle place," as he calls it, between remembering and anticipating. Having explored the "present of things past" in the first nine books, he is trying in the final books to explore the "present of things present" or "what now [he is] at the very time of making these confessions" (206).

Augustine's conversion has turned him around to himself, disclosing such pattern in his life as to rescue it from formless vagrancy. In turning to memory and time in Books Ten and Eleven, he will examine the means by which the narrative of his past has been available to him. He will take a phenomenological look, in other words, at the experience of his experience. Even for access to the present self, Augustine must turn to the memory without which, as he says: "I cannot so much as name myself." All of his life—past, present, and imagined future—is stored in the memory, even the past he has forgotten.

The room in the self for God, and in God for the self, is memory. God's memory, we might recall, preserves the time of Augustine's infancy, the time before speech and therefore predating Augustine's own memory. As a result, even that unconscious time is accessible to Augustine's autobiographical recovery of his past. Past time is never *temps perdu.* In the surety of that faith, he can dare to announce in Book Ten, "I will confess then what I know of myself; I will confess also what I know not of myself" (208). But he continues nonetheless to call on God to "slay my emptiness" (231).

The books on memory and time are together a companion piece to the opening prayer in Augustine's continuing effort to locate God. He shifts from the cosmos of creation to the cosmos of memory, whose "manifoldness" is "deep and boundless." In this "vast cavern" the ingredients of the created world are translated, combined, and, since the memory is "the belly of the mind," digested. And it is here that Augustine meets up with God: "See what a space I have gone over in my memory seeking Thee, O Lord; and I have not found Thee, without it. Nor have I found anything concerning Thee, but what I have kept in my memory . . ." (226). Since Augustine must conclude from this negative evidence—the fact that God cannot be found outside the memory—that his memory is the container of God, he reengages the logic of his earlier questioning about God's location, asking now what place God occupies in his memory. But when he puts the problem of location in this way, he must conclude that there is "no place" that lodges God: "Place there is none; we go backward and forward, and there is no place" (227). Just as he will be unable to explain time when he is asked to define it, he is unable to explain to himself where God can be found in his memory for there is nowhere he can step back. Any "where" he can imagine is already in time and memory. The question, then, still remains: "And how shall I find Thee, if I remember Thee not?" (220).

The question is a rhetorical one, but it is not merely rhetorical; in itself the question constitutes the only answer that is true to Augustine's actual experience. His knowledge of God can follow only from his experience of Him. Although the self is not coextensive with the being of God, that being is finally inaccessible outside of the self that remembers. Augustine can seek only what he already in some sense knows, as the opening paragraphs of the *Confessions* make clear: "for who can call on Thee, not knowing Thee? for he that knoweth Thee not, may call on Thee as other than Thou art." (1) The antecedent knowledge of God that makes it possible for Augustine to call upon Him is not to be construed as an emanation of Ideal Form eternally stored in some universal memory. Rather it is the particular knowledge of a God who has insinuated Himself in Augustine's life, turning and twisting that life and finally discovering him to himself. To be sure, we find the ghost of Plato in the conception of God as the unchanging container of the universe, a conception that had become a theological cliché by the time of the *Confessions*. But that static view of God's perfection is held in tension with the living God of history, a tension that reflects the all but seamless coexistence of Greek and Hebrew thought in the classical Christian culture of the fourth and fifth centuries.

It is a tension, moreover, that is grounded in the experience of Augustine's life as lived, an experience that is as much a part of the last books of the *Confessions* as it is of the narrative recollection in the first nine. When critics, either literary or theological, argue that Augustine must relinquish hold on the ropes of his own experience-in-time in order to float free in some realm of timeless wisdom, they are reducing the *sapientia* of autobiographical standpoint to the *scientia* of worldless knowledge.

There is no way Augustine can get behind or outside his experience to posit God's existence, just as there is no way he can step outside of time in order to define it as an object. The passing of time is, finally, the irreducible fact of experience. Far from relinquishing his autobiographical standpoint in order to free his knowledge of self from historical time and space, Augustine secures that standpoint in the phenomenology of experience that Books Ten and Eleven comprise. Time is not the adversary of the self, as so much autobiography theory and essentialist theology assume. Time is the very medium of selfhood, since it makes possible the interrelatedness of experience which makes self-knowledge possible at all.

Who is God save *our* God? What is time save *our* time? God "is," but as the God who is remembered; time exists, but as the time that measures our lives. Without the first-person possessive—a first-person *plural* possessive, I hasten to add—the words have no meaning, since meaning is always a product of understanding, and understanding is grounded in and made possible by commitment: *credo ut intelligam!*

In what is surely the most familiar line of the *Confessions,* Augustine declares, ". . . our heart is restless, until it repose in Thee." He returns to the idea of rest at the end of Book Thirteen, this time as an attribute of God's being: ". . . Thy rest is Thou Thyself." Augustine reaches his goal of repose, but not a static repose of god-like perfection. "Our rest is our place"—so Augustine writes near the end of Book Thirteen. As if to make clear the fact that "place" is residential in the time-space of bodily human involvement, he immediately introduces the force of gravity to which any "spiritual" notion of human being would not be subject: "The body by its own weight strives towards its own place" (315). Augustine does not hover over his life in some timeless space above it. He comes to a landing in a life with its own particulars—a pear tree, a protective mother, a bastard son, a rhetorician's interest in language—and with its specific involvement in a world of conflicting allegiances and orthodoxies. A docetic flight to the Everywhere and the All-time would deprive him, after all, of the very life that has brought him to himself and God. The reality of his life as lived and confessed—this autobiographical experience is the "weight" that pulls and holds him to his place. Only by acknowledging the anchorage of this place is the autobiographer free to move on. In Augustine's words: "My weight is my love; thereby am I borne, withersoever I am borne" (315).

In moving backwards to the late fourth century of the *Confessions* from the mid-nineteenth and early twentieth-century works that have helped me to define the autobiographical situation, I found that a certain kind of accessibility, and not inaccessibility, presented the initial problem of understanding Augustine's text. Notwithstanding certain anachronisms of language and concept, the *Confessions* comes as a work which can too facilely be located and made sense of. What makes it strangely familiar is a double tradition which links our "now" with its "then": that tradition of both autobiography theory and theology which is characterized by a belief in static essences. In the case of autobiography, this belief finds expression in what I have defined as classical autobiography theory which posits a "true" self that is hidden, changeless, and finally ineffable. In the case of the theological tradition which seems to familiarize the *Confessions* for us, we find a concept of God (again: hidden, changeless, and finally ineffable) that constitutes little more than a mirror image of the essentialist self of classical autobiography theory. These traditions coalesce in the gnostic aestheticism to which a number of critics have consigned the *Confessions* in their efforts to claim this text for autobiography. It is from this consignment I have wanted to rescue the text in order to do two things: to establish more adequate grounds for the *Confessions'* membership in the genre of autobiography, and, further, to claim that the religious hermeneutic of *credo ut intelligam,* restored to temporality, can be paradigmatic of all acts of autobiography, indeed, of all interpretive activity. The "I" that understands is the "I" that is *committed* to understanding; the "I" that believes is the "I" that belongs. To belong is not to be fixed or even to be unquestioningly "at home" in a world. After all, it is this very fixedness and harmony which Thoreau, Wordsworth, and Proust finally reject; it is also this ahistorical (and Platonic) view of things that Augustine's exegesis of *Genesis* must undercut if, as the doctrine of creation *ex nihilo* implies, human "natality"—to use Hannah Arendt's word—is to be taken seriously as a real beginning and not simply as a pre-ordained event in a larger, already completed scheme.[12]

Interestingly enough, it is something like this all-encompassing scheme which for Georges Gusdorf (otherwise a consistent spokesman for classical autobiography theory) must be dissolved to make way for the emergence of autobiography. What he calls "the mythic framework of traditional teachings" must be displaced by "the perilous domain of history."[13] Gusdorf goes on to argue rightly that historical understanding had itself to change from the positivistic assumption that the historian could take a candid shot of the past without so much as an adjustment of the lens, to an appreciation of the contribution the historian's own perspective makes to the "facts" of history. But when he makes the further claim that "[t]he objective space of history is always a projection of the mental space of the historian,"[14] he has simply substituted a subjectivist essentialism, which relocates "truth" from outside to inside, for the objectivist essentialism he began by questioning. Gusdorf has moved us from an historical positivism to an aesthetical positivism which equates the truth with the interior harmony the self creates rather than discovers "out there." Transpersonal myth (in the Kermode sense of "paradigmatic rigidity") has been replaced by the personal myth Gusdorf mistakes for autobiography. What we end up with is autobiography's distortion as ideology—the self's takeover of the world, not an orientation within it. Selfhood is discovered not in its world but "from the other side of the mir-

12. See Arendt's discussion of natality or "real beginning" in *The Life of the Mind: Willing* (New York: Harcourt Brace Jovanovich, 1978), pp. 108–10.

13. Georges Gusdorf, "Conditions and Limits of Autobiography," in James Olney, ed., *Autobiography: Essays Theoretical and Critical* (Princeton: Princeton University Press, 1980), p. 30.

14. Ibid., p. 45.

ror."[15] The severance of *autos* from *bios* is complete; the alienation of *stade du miroir* is assured. The self belongs to nothing outside the infinitely elastic boundaries of its own consciousness, accountable only to its private and existential sense of truth and stylistic *justesse.*

Self, or rather, an *idea* of self, has been won, but nothing less than the world has been lost, the "common world" or the *sensus communis* without which we can have no sense of reality at all and, therefore, no possibility of self-realization. More than any writer of our time, Hannah Arendt appreciated the fact that selfhood has no meaning whatsoever outside of the shared notion of a common world. What is shared is not a common perspective on this world as though everyone occupied the same time and space. Rather, the full dimensionality of any particular object is guaranteed *because* each person sees from a time and place different from anyone else. Knowing that another can or might or has seen what is currently hidden from my view in any given moment frees me from having to race to the other side to check out its existence. In Arendt's words: ". . . the reality of the common world can be guaranteed only when, from their multiple positions and viewpoints, men [and women] declare themselves to be holding the same object in view. If the sameness of the object can no longer be discerned, then nothing can prevent its destruction. . . . [T]he end of the common world has come when it is seen only under one aspect and is permitted to present itself only in one perspective."[16] What classical autobiographical theory overlooks is the fact that my own view of myself (from the other side of the mirror) means little without the other's view of me and, concommitantly, my view of the other. It is possible to claim, of course, that autobiography portrays both views at

15. Ibid., p. 35.
16. Hannah Arendt, *The Human Condition* (Chicago: University of Chicago Press, 1958), p. 58.

the same time, in an act that defies the force of gravity and the limits of space and time. To portray autobiography as such a solipsistic act is to resign the self to a silent and lifeless "world"—a "world," finally, devoid of self as well as others, since the differentiating circumstances of time and space would be collapsed into a single all-inclusive consciousness which would have nothing to be conscious of except Itself. Was it not in such a non-place that Narcissus drowned?

Augustine's *Confessions* makes emphatic the undeniable role of the *other* in the self's journey to realization. Beginning as it does with the autobiographer's impassioned address, the work dramatizes a self whose reality depends not only on reception but also on response from that other. The self's narrative starts with a relationship between itself and the other already in motion. Whatever comes *before* this relation is "narratable" only from the standpoint of the relation: through a process of retrospection, not cause and effect. The self's need of the other for its reality is made even more dramatic when, in Books Twelve and Thirteen, it becomes clear that the recipient of and respondent to the self's question is also the creator of the self who asks the questions.

While the *Confessions* begins with the self's sense of belonging, even if that belonging is expressed in the form of questions, much modern autobiography begins with the self's sense of loss or of being out of relation with something. More accurately, modern autobiography can be said to occupy a place between losing and finding, a liminal space where what has been lost can only be recalled and what might be possible, only anticipated. Especially alluring for autobiography in such an in-between place is a temptation toward nostalgia. To succumb to this temptation would contribute not at all to self-realization, since autobiography would rest on two illusions: the illusion that the self can somehow reverse its forward trajectory in order to leap backwards, and the further illusion that, were it able to eject itself from temporality, the self would find some unspoiled Eden (the "enchanted realm" of childhood) awaiting its arrival. Corollary to the nostalgic pull towards a perfect past is the allure of utopian imagination, which must ignore both the past and the *nunc stans* of the present in its catapult into some illusory future devoid of all tenses.

An example of autobiographical writing that might be accused of succumbing to both temptations is *Black Elk Speaks,* a memoiristic account which records the breaking-up of the traditional world of a native American and his increasingly desperate attempt to put that world back together again. In accounting for the steadily increasing popularity of the book—first published in 1932, reissued in 1961, and translated into eight languages by 1972 when it went into mass publication—one critic suggests that it "speak[s] to the twentieth-century yearning for simpler times and a more coherent universe."[17] It might be said, then, that Black Elk's attempt to recover the power of his remarkable boyhood vision, the explicitly religious center of the book, addresses this more universal yearning for a golden past. It might also be said that the book feeds the twentieth-century's concomitant and surprisingly persistent belief in progress when, in later portions, the Indians' growing desperation lends urgency to the "Messiah Craze" which promised a glorious future.

Moreover, it would certainly be possible to deny the work any autobiographical status at all, since the authorship of the story is so problematic. Not only is authorship shared with, and in certain sections taken over by, John G. Neihardt, a poet-anthropologist to whom the old Indian was willing to reveal his power-vision; the story is filtered

17. Sally McClusky, *"Black Elk Speaks:* and So Does John Neihardt," *Western American Literature* VI (1972): 231.

through Black Elk's son, who acted as interpreter for his non-English-speaking father, and through Neihardt's daughter, whose stenographic notes provided the father the basis for his editing. Moreover, the voices in the account itself are many, with the autobiographically unconventional breaking in of other first-persons who tell their own stories. And even now, there are reported grumblings from Oglala Sioux tribesmen who accuse Black Elk of fobbing off their stories as his own.

Or, it might be argued, if the work is in any sense autobiographical, *Black Elk Speaks* must fall into the category of failed autobiography, since the old Indian was unable to recover the vision or to put back together the pieces of a self and its world which had been shattered and scattered by the alien forces of history. The book ends with these poignant words:

> And so it was all over.
>
> I did not know then how much was ended. When I look back now from this high hill of my old age, I can still see the butchered women and children lying heaped and scattered all along the crooked gulch as plain as when I saw them with eyes still young. And I can see that something else died there in the bloody mud, and was buried in the blizzard. A people's dream died there. It was a beautiful dream.
>
> And I, to whom so great a vision was given in my youth,—you see me now a pitiful old man who has done nothing, for the nation's hoop is broken and scattered. There is no center any longer, and the sacred tree is dead.[18]

18. Black Elk, *Black Elk Speaks: Being the Life Story of a Holy Man of the Oglala Sioux as told through John G. Neihardt* (Lincoln: University of Nebraska Press, 1961), p. 276. Subsequent citations will be indicated by page numbers following the quotation in my text.

Unlike the Augustinian journey of selfhood, during which the initially scattered pieces are collected and re-collected along the way, Black Elk's journey moves from a world of shared and coherent values to fragmentation, a valley of dry bones which the most powerful of spirits cannot infuse again with their former life. Black Elk moves, in other words, to the periphery where things, as William Butler Yeats said of another shattered world, could no longer hold together. In the face of this conclusion, one might argue that *Black Elk Speaks* illustrates the failure of the very task of autobiography: to find a life's pattern and meaning.

But rather than dismissing *Black Elk Speaks* as exemplary of what true autobiography is *not*, I want to make the opposite case. Different as it is from the personally crafted works of literary culture I used to define the three moments of the autobiographical situation, and distant though this work may seem to be from the affirmation of place which centers and unites the Augustinian self with its lived past, *Black Elk Speaks* secures for autobiography the essential *worldliness* of the genre. A term of Hannah Arendt's, I use it to reinforce the nature of true autobiography as an act of plural, not singular, reflexivity and as an act of display or a performance.

Self-realization demands a world in which the self is known by others. Being known by others (or, for Augustine, by *the* Other) is prior to self-knowledge. Arendt goes even further: Who I am is something *only* others can know since to myself I am opaque. The world is constituted and guaranteed by selves appearing to, not hiding from, one another. To be sure, the self's appearing, its performance or display, can be misunderstood. Nonetheless the self must be *taken to be* this or that, rightly or wrongly, in order to be at all. The self must be interpreted, then, or read by others —not as a text complete in itself with a single, unchanging, and transparent meaning, but as a text that requires continuing interpretation in order to mean at all. The self cannot be defined as being-once-and-for-all. Rather the self goes on being: in the words of a Bob Dylan song, it "keeps on keeping on."

Black Elk Speaks enacts the features of true autobiography in several ways. The well-known fact of its multiple authorship—which, from the perspective of classical autobiography theory, gives just cause for dismissal from the autobiographical tradition—simply makes explicit what is tacitly always the case in every autobiography. If self-realization must be gained from the ways the self is known by others, authorship of autobiography, in effect, is always multiple. The story told through the convention of first-person narrative is always a story which both discovers and creates the relation of self with the world in which it can appear to others, knowing itself only in that appearance or display.[19] This aspect of autobiography's worldliness is to be seen in the first page of Black Elk's story when he offers an account of who he is and why he can tell this story:

> My friend, I am going to tell you the story of my life, as you wish; and if it were only the story of my life I think I would not tell it; for what is one man that he

19. The relational character of self-knowledge can be seen in *Walden* as well as in the Wordsworth poems, *Remembrance of Things Past* and the autobiographical writing of Augustine and Black Elk. Self-realization is made possible for Thoreau in the *language* of nature, not nature itself. Moreover, when Thoreau sets out to find the origins of language in Nature, he discovers that it is language—a *social* and *intersubjective* phenomenon—that must mediate his relation with Nature, i.e., reality. I have already noted the role of the "other" in the Wordsworth poems (the Leech-gatherer, whose limiting and defining presence saves the poet from the madness of solipsism; and the figure of Dorothy, through whom the poet experiences the full dimensionality of his temporal placing); and in *Remembrance of Things Past* (the "true mirror" of Marcel's selfhood being provided by the eyes of the aging characters at the afternoon party).

should make much of his winters, even when they
bend him like a heavy snow. . . . It is the story of all
life that is holy and is good to tell, and of us two-
leggeds sharing in it with the four-leggeds and the
wings of the air and all green things; for these are
children of one mother and their father is one Spirit (1).

This ecological version of selfhood must be seen in
tension with the self bereft of its world that comes through
in the final paragraph of the book. Both versions must be
seen as distinct from the extreme individualism of the "black
road" Black Elk recalls from his power-vision where, near
the end of the story, he sees his vanquished people travelling:
"everyone for himself and with little rules of his own" (219).
Everything he relates to Neihardt is being spoken, after all,
from the retrospective standpoint of that lonely hill of his
old age *after* he and his people have been displaced from
"the mythic framework of traditional teachings" to "the
perilous domain of history." Like the modern autobiographer, this erstwhile traditional man occupies a place between his loss and his finding, a space he fills with his
speaking.

Yet another instance of the relational character of autobiography can be noted in the Sacred Pipe story Black Elk
shares with Neihardt at the beginning of the account. The
story tells of a "sacred woman" appearing to two scouts
whose minds she could read and one of whom she turned
into a "skeleton covered with worms" (4). The other she
instructs to return in order to prepare his people for her
coming to them with the sacred pipe. The story is full of the
miraculous and the imagery that will figure prominently in
the power-vision Black Elk will be telling soon to Neihardt.
The Sacred Pipe story prepares the way for more than the
account of his boyhood vision, however. Like the passing of
the pipe, which took place between Black Elk and his co-

author at the outset of their meeting, the Sacred Pipe story sets a communal and fiduciary context for the telling of the former's story as well as for Neihardt's response and, eventually, for his translation-interpretation of Black Elk's life into written language that makes his life explicit. Black Elk's comment at the end of the Pipe story is especially striking in this regard. "This they tell," he remarks, "and whether it happened so or not I do not know; but if you think about it, you can see that it is true" (5). Truth lies in the story's *sufficiency:* in its capacity to make sense of experience told, shared, and even made newly possible for both the teller and the hearer of the story. Just as the authorship of autobiography is tacitly plural, so the truth of autobiography is to be found, not in the "facts" of the story itself, but in the relational space *between* the story and its reader.

Connected to the relational or plural character of autobiography's worldliness is the self's display, which contradicts the assumption of classical autobiographical theory that the true self, hidden and private, must sell out when it shows itself to the world in the distorting form of language. To expose the fallacy of this essentialist argument, Hannah Arendt uses the work of the Swiss zoologist Adoph Portmann, whose new "morphology" of vertebrates serves to reverse the old "metaphysical hierarchy" which devalues surface in favor of depth. Simply put, Portmann suggests that very few besides the specialist could tell the difference between the interior skeletal structures, say, of the vulture and the peacock. There is no mistaking the difference, however, in the ways they *display* themselves.[20] Arendt uses this striking argument, about the relative contributions that depth and surface make to "true" identity, as support for her larger contention about the "primacy of appearances." In

20. See Arendt's use of Portmann's work in *The Life of the Mind: Thinking* (New York: Harcourt Brace Jovanovich, 1978), pp. 26–30.

her effort to undermine the widespread notion that depth as the cause of surface is therefore ontologically superior, she says, while "there may indeed exist a fundamental ground behind an appearing world, . . . this ground's chief and even sole significance lies in its effects, that is, in what it causes to appear."[21]

Black Elk and his tribe put this basic pragmatic insight into action when they collaborate in the performance of the former's power-vision. The performance—when other Indians were assigned the roles and made up to resemble the host of persons and animals Black Elk experienced in the vision itself—does not take place until years after he had had the private vision at nine years of age. He carried the memory of that vision with him, claiming it remembered itself, but it did not become powerful or really real until it was "tribalized": until it was shared with and displayed for the community. Only then, when the vision made its appearance in the world, and indeed, helped to create that world, was it possible to understand its meaning. What Black Elk remarks about another ceremony applies to this one as well: "It is from understanding that power comes; and the power in the ceremony was in understanding what it meant. . ." (212).

There is yet another performance to be noted—for my purposes, the most important one. This is the narrative performance of *Black Elk Speaks*, itself representing a display which Neihardt, in first hearing the old Indian's words, compares with "half seeing, half sensing a strange and beautiful landscape by brief flashes of sheet lightning."[22] While Black Elk ended that display by lamenting the failure of his vision, he had been formidably successful in performing the vision of his very life to Neihardt and eventually to the new

21. Ibid., p. 42.
22. John Neihardt, "The Book That Would Not Die," *Western American Literature* VI (1972): 228.

world of its readership. Paradoxically, this readership numbers among its members the descendents of those "Wasi-
chus" who expropriated Black Elk's sacred landscape.

That autobiography, too, can be an act of expropriat-
ing rather than appropriating meaning cannot be denied.
Interpretation has its risks: the risk of drowning, like Narcissus, in ideological certainty; or the risk of being strangled in
the air by some brand of Herculean deconstruction when,
like Antaeus, the autobiographer loses contact with the
"spot of time" which grounds his or her life, and *autos* is
severed from *bios*.

Thoreau issues a warning about these risks in the anecdote that helps to conclude his autobiographical excursion.
A comic version of the Narcissus myth, his is a story about
a traveller, a boy, and a swamp:

> We read that the traveller asked the boy if the swamp
> before him had a hard bottom. The boy replied that it
> had. But presently the traveller's horse sank in up to the
> girths, and he observed to the boy, "I thought you said
> that this bog had a hard bottom." "So it has," answered
> the latter, "but you have not got half way to it yet"
> (330).

Thoreau makes clear the allegorical intent of the anecdote: "So it is," he suggests, "with the bogs and quicksands
of society; but he is an old boy that knows it" (330). The
allegory can be extended as well to the bogs and quicksands
of interpretive activity—not only to the risks of autobiographical reading, but to the risks of reading any text. In
either case, there is the problem of recovering meaning and,
prior to that, of locating truth.

Is truth located in an originating situation that lies
behind a facade or, in the terms of Thoreau's anecdote,
below the surface? Such would seem to be the case in that

understanding of autobiography which defines the self as a private and, finally, transcendent modality unaffected by (because unaffiliated with) culture. For these theorists, there is, indeed, a hard bottom, and it is possible (and necessary) to wedge through cultural accretions to the deep structures which constitute truth.

Although it was such a wedging strategy that Thoreau initially announced for his experiment, it is also his autobiographical excursion that finally calls it into question. The *"point d'appui"* he wanted to secure turns out to have its liabilities. In reaching the bottom "with rocks in place" and to call this arrival "reality" is to run the risk of Narcissus and drown in certainty. Moreover, this Archemedean strategy runs counter to that temporality which characterizes all interpretive activity and, in fact, makes it possible at all. Neither the past nor the present simply stays put.

Throughout *Walden,* Thoreau employs the image of the traveller to portray the writer's career. The image also applies to the reader who perforce interprets as a transient.[23] While travelling has its pleasures of discovery and rediscovery, it runs the risk of premature or false destination, as the swamp story humorously suggests. In light of this latter possibility, the constraints against our ever reaching bottom, as Frank Kermode wants to remind the critic in *The Genesis of Secrecy,* are reassuring as well as limiting. "No one," Kermode says, "however special his point of vantage, can get past all those doorkeepers [of culture, convention, ideology, and so on] into the shrine of the single sense."[24]

The opacity that always characterizes our relation to the past, to texts, and, more than that, to the world, *fuels* interpretation; it enjoins us to have it out with the world in

23. See Frank Kermode on the transiency of interpretive activity in *The Genesis of Secrecy: On the Interpretation of Narrative* (Cambridge: Harvard University Press, 1979), p. 145.
24. Ibid., p. 123.

sense-making activity that secures our collusion with the world, marking us as human and cultural beings whose meanings are implicated in our worldliness. Further, the possibility of loss, no less than the prospects for recovery, make of autobiography (or any act of interpretation) the *vital* activity that it is. The self which autobiography performs is the self who forgets as well as remembers, the self who dies as well as lives. It is the self that comes up against its limits, most especially the limit of the other by virtue of which and only in relation to which the self knows *who* and *where* it is and thereby becomes "fierce with reality."[25]

25. See epigraph for Chapter 1.

Selected Bibliography

I include in the following list only the books and essays that fall outside the definitive bibliography on autobiography recently provided by James Olney in *Autobiography: Essays Theoretical and Critical* (Princeton, 1980), pp. 343–52. By excluding recognized sources for autobiography study (many of which I have used and noted elsewhere in this book), I want to highlight the kinds of ideas, methods, and issues which I found most distinctively useful in developing my own approach to the genre. Of the items listed below, the most fundamental (in addition to the primary autobiographical texts which furnished occasions for reflecting on genre questions) are the ones authored by Hannah Arendt, Hans-Georg Gadamer, E. H. Gombrich, Frank Kermode, Maurice Merleau-Ponty, José Ortega y Gasset, and Paul Ricoeur.

Altieri, Charles. "The Qualities of Action: A Theory of Middles in Literature." *Boundary 2* V (Spring 1977): 323–50.
——. "The Qualities of Action: Part II." *Boundary 2* V (Fall 1977): 899–917.
Arendt, Hannah. *The Human Condition.* Chicago: University of Chicago Press, 1958.
——. *The Life of the Mind: Thinking.* New York: Harcourt Brace Jovanovich, 1978.
——. *The Life of the Mind: Willing.* New York: Harcourt Brace Jovanovich, 1978.

Bachelard, Gaston. *The Poetics of Space*. Trans. Maria Jolas. New York: Orion Press, 1964.

Berthoff, Warner. *Fictions and Events: Essays in Criticism and Literary History*. New York: E. P. Dutton & Co., Inc., 1971.

Bloom, Harold. *The Map of Misreading*. New York: Oxford University Press, 1975.

Calinescu, Matei. "Hermeneutics or Poetics." *The Journal of Religion* LIX (January 1979): 1–17.

Cohn, Dorrit. *Transparent Minds: Narrative Modes for Presenting Consciousness in Fiction*. Princeton: Princeton University Press, 1978.

Crites, Stephen. "The Narrative Quality of Experience." *Journal of the American Academy of Religion* XXXIX (September 1971): 291–311.

Eliade, Mircea. *Cosmos and History: The Myth of the Eternal Return*. Trans. Willard R. Trask. New York: Harper & Brothers, 1959.

Fish, Stanley. "Literature in the Reader: Affective Stylistics." *New Literary History* II (Autumn 1970): 123–62.

Frank, Joseph. "Spatial Form in Modern Literature." In *The Widening Gyre: Crisis and Mastery in Modern Literature*. Bloomington: Indiana University Press, 1968.

Gadamer, Hans-Georg. *Philosophical Hermeneutics*. Trans. and ed. by David Linge. Berkeley: University of California Press, 1977.

————. *Truth and Method*. Translation edited by Garrett Barden and John Cumming. A Continuum Book. New York: The Seabury Press, 1975.

Geertz, Clifford. *The Interpretation of Cultures*. New York: Basic Books, 1973.

Gombrich, E. H. *Art and Illusion: A Study in the Psychology of Pictorial Representation*. Bollingen Series XXXV, 5. Princeton: Princeton University Press, 1972.

Grene, Marjorie. *The Knower and the Known*. Berkeley: University of California Press, 1974.

Hardy, Barbara. *Tellers and Listeners: The Narrative Imagination*. London: The Athlone Press, 1975.

Hirsch, E. D. *Validity in Interpretation.* New Haven: Yale University Press, 1963.

Holland, Norman. *The Dynamics of Literary Response.* New York: Oxford University Press, 1968.

Iser, Wolfgang. *The Implied Reader: Patterns of Communication in Prose Fiction from Bunyan to Beckett.* Baltimore: The Johns Hopkins University Press, 1974.

Josipovici, Gabriel. *The World and the Book: A Study of Modern Fiction.* Stanford: Stanford University Press, 1971.

Kermode, Frank. *The Genesis of Secrecy: On the Interpretation of Narrative.* Cambridge: Harvard University Press, 1979.

_____. *The Sense of an Ending: Studies in the Theory of Fiction.* New York: Oxford University Press, 1967.

Merleau-Ponty, M[aurice]. *Phenomenology of Perception.* Trans. Colin Smith. London: Routledge & Kegan Paul, 1962.

_____. *Sense and Non-Sense.* Trans. Hubert L. Dreyfus and Patricia Allen Dreyfus. Evanston: Northwestern University Press, 1964.

_____. *Signs.* Trans. Richard C. McCleary. Evanston: Northwestern University Press, 1964.

_____. *The Visible and the Invisible.* Ed. Claude Lefort. Trans. Alphonso Lingis. Evanston: Northwestern University Press, 1968.

Ortega y Gasset, José. *Concord and Liberty.* Trans. Helene Weyl. New York: W. W. Norton & Co. Inc., 1946.

_____. *History as a System and Other Essays Toward a Philosophy of History.* New York: W. W. Norton & Co., 1961.

_____. *Meditations on Quixote.* Trans. Evelyn Rugg and Diego Marin. New York: W. W. Norton & Co., 1961.

_____. *The Modern Temper.* Trans. James Cleugh. New York: Harper & Row, 1961.

_____. *Phenomenology and Art.* Trans. Philip W. Silver. New York: W. W. Norton & Co., Inc., 1975.

Plumb, J. H. *The Death of the Past.* Boston: Houghton Mifflin Co., 1971.

Polanyi, Michael. *Personal Knowledge: Towards a Post-Critical Philosophy.* Chicago: University of Chicago Press, 1974.

_____. *The Tacit Dimension.* Garden City, N. Y.: Doubleday & Co., 1966.

Ricoeur, Paul. *Interpretation Theory: Discourse and the Surplus of Meaning.* Fort Worth: The Texas Christian University Press, 1976.

_____. *The Rule of Metaphor: Multi-Disciplinary Studies of the Creation of Meaning in Language.* Trans. Robert Czerny, with Kathleen McLaughlin and John Costello. Toronto: University of Toronto Press, 1977.

_____. *The Symbolism of Evil.* Trans. Emerson Buchanan. New York: Harper & Row., 1967.

Spencer, Sharon. *Space, Time, and Structure in the Modern Novel.* New York: New York University Press, 1971.

Smith, Barbara Herrnstein. *On the Margins of Discourse: The Relation of Literature to Language.* Chicago: University of Chicago Press, 1978.

Trilling, Lionel. *Sincerity and Authenticity.* Cambridge: Harvard University Press, 1972.

White, Hayden. *Tropics of Discourse: Essays in Cultural Criticism.* Baltimore: The Johns Hopkins University Press, 1978.

Index